THE MASTER'S WIFE

SIR ANDREW MACPHAIL

THE MASTER'S WIFE

SIR ANDREW MACPHAIL

With an Introduction by
Ian Ross Robertson

Institute of Island Studies
CHARLOTTETOWN
1994

©1994, The Institute of Island Studies
Introduction ©Ian Ross Robertson, 1994
ISBN 0-919013-21-X

Facsimile of 1939 Edition
Published by Jeffrey Macphail and Dorothy Lindsay, Montreal

Cover design and additional book design by Ken Shelton
Project co-ordination by Laurie Brinklow
Printed and bound in Canada by Williams & Crue Ltd.,
    Summerside, Prince Edward Island
Cover and back cover photo courtesy
    The Sir Andrew Macphail Foundation

Published with the kind assistance of
    The Sir Andrew Macphail Foundation and
    The Prince Edward Island Council of the Arts and
    the Department of Education and Human Resources

Second printing 2001, with funding from Diagnostic Chemicals Ltd.

Canadian Cataloguing in Publication Data

Macphail, Andrew, Sir, 1864-1938.

    The Master's Wife

    Facsim. reprint. Originally published: Montreal:
J. Macphail and D. Lindsay, 1939.
    ISBN 0-919013-21-X

1. Macphail, Andrew, Sir, 1864-1938. 2. Macphail,
Catherine, 1834-1920. 3. Orwell (P.E.I.) -- Social
life and customs. 4. Orwell (P.E.I.) -- Biography.
I. University of Prince Edward Island. Institute of
Island Studies. II. Title

FC2649.078Z49 1994 C818'.5203 C94-950222-7
F1049.5.078M32 1994

To

Jeffrey and Dorothy

"Good Children"

LIST OF ILLUSTRATIONS

Cover   The Master's Wife, 1919
Frontispiece   Sir Andrew Macphail
Between pages 32 and 33   The Master, 1860
Between pages 52 and 53   The Master, 1899
Between pages 76 and 77   The Grandmother
Between pages 128 and 129   Coleshill (psalm in Gaelic)
Between pages 226 and 227   The Master's Wife, 1919
Back cover   Andrew Macphail, 1897

CONTENTS

"The Spirit" - viii
Preface - ix
Introduction - xi

    I. IN THE BEGINNING - 1
   II. THE SPAR-MAKER - 6
  III. HER PEOPLE - 16
  IV. THE IMMIGRANTS - 26
   V. THE NEW WORLD - 37
  VI. THE MASTER HIMSELF - 52
 VII. THE WORLD OF SIN - 63
VIII. HIS MOTHER - 73
  IX. THE OLD HOUSE - 87
   X. THE ECONOMY OF THE HOUSE - - - - - - - - - - - - - - 98
  XI. THE WRITTEN WORD - 110
 XII. THE TWO RACES - 121
XIII. THE WORLD OF RELIGION - - - - - - - - - - - - - - - - - - 126
XIV. THE WORLD OF NATURE - - - - - - - - - - - - - - - - - - 153
 XV. THE OPEN DOOR - 159
XVI. THE ESCAPE - 174
XVII. HER HUMANITY - 189
XVIII. THE TWO HORSES - 201
XIX. THE MUSICIANS - 210
 XX. THE TWO PRINCES - 222
XXI. THE SPIRIT OF WAR - 228
XXII. FALSE PRIDE - 239

Explanatory Notes - 249
Corrigenda - 254

THE SPIRIT

There is a winding path that curves through
A little green and lovely wood with trees
That softly sway, led by the gentle breeze.
Along it slowly moves a man - but who?
And nearer and nearer draws the man, but as
He closer comes, he seems to fade, to grow
So misty dim, a fleeting shadow.
Ah yes, it is the spirit and it has
Been wandering through that heavenly little wood
As essence ever since he died, for when
Alive, he loved this place, and now and then
He reappears, and then from where I stood
I saw him slowly come to shape and softly creep
Towards me. He said "Awake" and I awoke from sleep.

Jeffrey Burland Lindsay

PREFACE
to the Third Edition

THE present edition represents a homecoming for *The Master's Wife*, a classic of Prince Edward Island literature set in the Scottish community of Orwell. Published initially in Montreal in 1939 by Macphail's son and daughter, then in Toronto in 1977 in McClelland and Stewart's prestigious New Canadian Library Series, the book is now produced for the first time on the author's native Island.

In this facsimile edition, we have brought together two outstanding features of the previous versions - the handsome type and illustrations of the 1939 publication, and the authoritative Introduction which first appeared in the McClelland and Stewart edition. We are grateful to Frank and Juanita Lechowick of Charlottetown, who "sacrificed" a treasured copy of the original *The Master's Wife* to be taken apart for this photographic process; and to Macphail scholar Ian Ross Robertson who has updated and expanded his 1977 Introduction.

Dr. Robertson has also prepared a set of explanatory notes and *corrigenda* to accompany the text. These scholarly additions we have placed at the end of the book. It should be remembered that Sir Andrew Macphail died before the book was published, so that he had no opportunity to make a final check for typographical and other minor errors.

Original features of this edition include the sonnet "The Spirit" which appears on the facing page, as well as two photographs - that of Macphail on the back cover, and of his mother, "the Master's wife," which graces the front. For permission to use these we thank the Sir Andrew Macphail Foundation of Orwell. The poem was written by 14-year-old Jeffrey Burland Lindsay in 1938; it was a tribute to his grandfather, Sir Andrew, who had died earlier that year.

x

Finally, I want to stress what a privilege it is for the Institute of Island Studies to be able to publish this book. Without the active cooperation and support of the Macphail Foundation Board, this would not have been possible. Our special gratitude goes to Isabel Court, the Homestead Site Manager, and to Jack Pennock, whose enthusiasm set this project in motion. In recognition of the splendid work being done at Orwell, the Institute will donate to the Macphail Foundation an annual "tithe" of 10 per cent of total sales of this, the homecoming edition.

Harry Baglole, Director
Institute of Island Studies
University of Prince Edward Island

INTRODUCTION

THE *Master's Wife* is a semi-autobiographical portrait of life in a Scottish-Canadian rural community in the latter part of the 19th century. The district is Orwell, in south-eastern Prince Edward Island, and the author is Sir Andrew Macphail, a native of Orwell who went on to become a physician and writer in Montreal. The master of the title is Andrew's father, William McPhail,[1] a schoolmaster born in Scotland in 1830, who had been brought to British North America by his parents at the age of three; the master's wife is Andrew's mother, a native of nearby Lower Newtown. *The Master's Wife* has been referred to as a novel, apparently because of the novelistic technique of presentation through the mind of a child, which Macphail likens to "the mind of a dreamer by night." The characters, community, and events in *The Master's Wife* are real, yet by use of the free-associating perspective of the child and the unfettered movement through time - through decades upon decades in this case - allowed by dreams, "the whole figment," as Macphail writes, "has the force of intense reality." It also draws the reader in from the start with an unusual sensation of immediacy.

The book is a successful penetration into the inner life of a particular type of Scottish-Canadian community, and is a fund of information on its practices and world-view. An overwhelming proportion of the inhabitants of Orwell in Macphail's youth were Scottish by birth, or of Scottish-immigrant parentage. The way of life, religious customs, and hierarchy of values were those of the old country. As in Scotland, agriculture was unspecialized: the farmers grew oats, potatoes, wheat, barley, and turnips, and raised sheep, hogs, and cattle. Almost everyone was a Calvinist of one variety or another; the Macphails were "McDonaldites," a sect claiming connection

---

[1] As an adult, Andrew adopted the spelling "Macphail"; his father continued to use "McPhail."

xi

with the Church of Scotland, although in practice unique to the Island. When in 1869 William McPhail and his fellow-elders drafted a letter asking to be allowed to retain their pastor, they stated that the vast majority of their people were unilingual Gaelic-speaking Highlanders, requiring a Gaelic-speaking minister. But above all *The Master's Wife* excels in its portrayal of the Scottish-Canadian attitude to education; it was "the escape," the means of release from manual toil. He who could master the classics would never have to work with his hands. The school was for boys who could grasp that key, and part of the task of the master, or *dominie*, was to weed out those who could not. Consequently, the choice of a master was a serious matter, and, once he was chosen, the prestige of the master within the community was second only to that of the minister.

The Master's Wife was written as a celebration of this traditional way of life. Through skillful characterization and use of anecdote, Macphail conveys an appreciation of what it was like to be born and raised in such an atmosphere: the closeness of the family circle, cemented by the interdependent duties of each member, all performed on the same farm; the love of the animals and the sorrow attendant upon their slaughter; the pleasure in learning the many skills in which farm children had to become proficient; the omnipresence of religious sanctions; the long Sabbaths which could only be broken by going to a field with a hidden book, under pretence of solicitude for the grazing animals; the hint of an external world provided by a first taste of exotic, aromatic coffee, thanks to the Minister's wife, "a foreign woman, that is, from Nova Scotia"; the breaks in claustrophobic solemnity provided by the tales of a Scottish grandmother who delighted in thunderstorms and brandy, told of witches, and refused to take life entirely seriously, or by the visits of a seafaring uncle bearing wondrous gifts from abroad and "a breath of intelligence from the larger world"; and the love of company and generous hospitality that co-existed with faint suspicion of anyone from outside the community. Although the book is autobiographical, it is more than that. *The Master's Wife* is not a lament, but an almost joyous affirmation of the virtues and pleasures of Macphail's ancestral way of life, a point Maurice Lebel underscored when reviewing it in *Le Devoir*, 3 February 1940: "Ce livre renferme toute une philosophie de la vie. Il serait relativement facile d'en extraire toute une série de pensées profondes qui se lise comme des maximes. On sent que l'auteur y a condensé les résultats de son expérience du monde et des hommes."

Who was Andrew Macphail, and what did he bring to this book, which he worked on for at least ten years? Born "John Andrew McPhail" in September of 1864, shortly after the Charlottetown Conference, he completed the course of studies at Uigg Grammar School in the district neighbouring Orwell, and won a scholarship to attend Prince of Wales College in Charlottetown. This was an institution which trained teachers for the district schools of the province and prepared students for higher education elsewhere. The excellent teaching and classical ideals he encountered at Prince of Wales influenced him permanently. He taught for three years in rural Prince Edward Island, virtually all of that time in Malpeque, of which he writes fondly in *The Master's Wife*. Some 55 miles west of Orwell, it was in some respects, as he explains, a world away.

[T]he Master would have considered [Malpeque] a worldly place. It was the oldest settlement on the Island, rich, compact, and completely civilized. There was a handsome church, an educated minister, two services a day. If he had suggested that his congregation were "sinners," they would have received the news with polite amusement. An evangelist was regarded as a curiosity, as a diversion. One of these was much encouraged by the large attendance. He asked those who were "saved" to stand up. No one moved. Moderating his appeal, he asked those who "desired to be saved" to stand up. The result was no better. Then, with a touch of irony, he appealed to all who wished to lead a "better life." The only response was from a low fellow who was known to be a fool and was suspected of being a thief. "Happy people," the evangelist exclaimed, and abandoned that cultivated field.

They were happy people, shrewd, kind, fond of gaiety and jest; and the old took their pleasures with the young.

Macphail proceeded next to Montreal, where he attended McGill University between 1885 and 1891, receiving a BA and an MD. He had greatly underestimated living expenses there, and he was obliged to work as a private tutor and a journalist in order to supplement his savings. While he pursued his medical studies, he was also working full-time as a journalist for first the Montreal *Gazette*, where he was night editor, then the Montreal *Star*, where he was commercial editor, and then a wire service. Despite the heavy workload, "John A. McPhail," as he was known, became an important figure in extra-curricular student activities at McGill. For example, in 1890, at a university dinner he spoke on behalf of his medical class, with the governor-general, Lord Stanley (of "Stanley Cup" fame), the prime minister, Sir John Macdonald, and the leader of the opposition, Wilfrid Laurier, all present. Before his graduation, Macphail won an essay contest on vivisection sponsored by the American Humane Education Society, open to the English-speaking world, and juried by Harvard University medical professors. He defended the practice, irritating anti-vivisectionists, and provoking a tidal wave of hostile correspondence, which kept coming for years. By the time he graduated in medicine at age 26 he had demonstrated remarkable capacity for hard work, unusual versatility, and exceptional aptitude as a writer. After graduating, he took a world tour financed by a syndicate of Canadian and American newspapers in exchange for rights to the travel articles he wrote along the way.

After the trip and some further medical study in England, Macphail devoted his time primarily to medical practice for about ten years. He also taught in the medical faculty of the University of Bishop's College, Montreal (1893-1905), which eventually was absorbed by McGill. From 1907 until the year before his death in 1938 he was McGill's professor of the history of medicine. He had become editor of the *Montreal Medical Journal* in 1903, and when it merged with another journal eight years later to form the *Canadian Medical Association Journal*, he was the founding editor. It was characteristic of him that his first editorial in the national periodical was entitled "Style in Medical Writing."

In the meantime, Macphail had begun to write in a serious way on subjects other than medicine. He had married in 1893, and his wife died in 1902 at age 32. Her death appears to have been a turning-point for him: afterwards, he became much more interested in literature than ever before. His first project was the compilation of an anthology of poetry on the theme of sorrow, including two Petrarchan sonnets of his own; but he did not publish the book until 1916, in the midst of the First World War. He published his first volume of essays in 1905, produced a novel in 1906, wrote a play in 1914, translated the French-language novel *Maria Chapdelaine* in 1921, and composed a wide range of other works over four decades. Among them were a book on the Bible in Scotland, a long essay on the history of his native province for the multi-volume *Canada and its Provinces*, and the official history of the Canadian Army Medical Services during the First World War. He had served as a medical officer overseas, although an accident in 1911 had left him virtually blind in his left eye, and although he had turned 50 shortly after the war began. Historian J.M.Bumsted describes his medical history as "a classic analysis of the non-combative aspects of modern war."

At McGill, Macphail was one of the most vivid characters on campus. Stephen Leacock, the humourist and professor of political economy, was convinced that Macphail had been a truly distinctive individual. He knew, on the basis of his own observation, that Macphail had been endowed with a personality so strong that even famous people tended to defer to his wishes on first meeting. In Leacock's words,

> Andrew seemed so different to other men that his presence seemed to lift an occasion out of the commonplace. Introduced to strangers, he made an instant impression.

Those of us who had to entertain, in public or in private, a visiting celebrity at once sent for Andrew: just as one sends for the doctor; and no celebrity could "celebrity" him. He treated them as a man used to horses treats a new one. It always seemed amazing to me that he could handle them so easily. Rudyard Kipling came to Montreal. Andrew had him tamed in half an hour, took him over to his house and then put him upstairs to write a speech. "Has Kipling come?" asked a next entering visitor, in the awestruck tones we used for celebrities in the days before the Great War gave us our own. "He's upstairs," Andrew said, "I told him he ought to *write* his speech for McGill; he's writing it."

That was the beginning of an enduring friendship between the two men. When Macphail was on leave from service in the First World War, he usually visited with Kipling at his home in Sussex. In fact, all members of his family who were in England during the war - his daughter, his son, and his brother - were welcome there.

Although Macphail spent most of each year in Montreal, he remained in constant contact with his native district. After his wife's death he began to send his two small children to Orwell for the summer. Following the death of his father in 1905, he himself spent his entire summers there. An active man, he carried out a variety of agricultural experiments. It was an era when the population of Prince Edward Island was declining dramatically, as thousands of Islanders left for central Canada, or, more frequently, New England. Andrew and his brother Alexander, a professor of engineering at Queen's University in Kingston, hoped to demonstrate to interested Islanders how new crops could be developed, and how scientific methods could make farming viable once again. In addition to these activities, which were quite extensive, Andrew welcomed visitors to his summer retreat in Orwell. One of these, Archibald MacMechan, a professor of English literature at Dalhousie University in Halifax, portrayed the host in verse:

A close-lipped man; yea, somewhat saturnine;
A good deal of Mephisto in his air;
A red Satanic beard; cropt, scanty hair;
A forehead plowed by many a thoughtful line;
A Highland accent with a humorous whine;
A scholar's stoop; a disconcerting stare;
Inclined to stoutness (but he does not care);
And Highland legs to prop the whole design.

A Highland voice; and Highland courtesie;
A Highland welcome for the favoured guest,
Who visits him within his Island cell,
Embowered in lush potatoes, wild and free.
Mephisto - (may be!) - to advantage drest,
But Mr. Greatheart underneath the shell.

As an author, Macphail's favourite literary form was the essay, which displayed to good advantage his ability to craft the exact phrase to catch the reader's attention. Over the years he published scores of essays, and in fact four book-length collections of them. As Elspeth Cameron, a specialist in Canadian literature at the University of Toronto, has written in an article surveying the essay as a literary *genre* in Canada, Macphail's essays "were outstanding examples of the well-informed mind reflecting deeply on such issues as puritanism, the arts, Canada's national duty to England, religion, and women's role in society."

One of Macphail's most distinctive traits as a writer was clearly his breadth. In his period of prominence, he was the best Canadian personification of a certain 19th-century ideal of the scholar. This type has been identified as the "man-of-letters," who is distinguished from other members of the intelligentsia by his versatility and lack of an exclusive specialization; he tends to cover the ground of all the specialists. In the 20th century the man-of-letters has been a disappearing breed, particularly in the highly differentiated and specialized world of North America. More than any other Canadian writer, Macphail resisted this system of specialization, for he wrote in an informed way on almost everything from aesthetics to science. In the field of his greatest distinction, social criticism, he articulated a remarkably comprehensive and well-integrated world-view, and in this respect his medical training had probably exerted a decisive influence. With its emphasis upon seeing the patient as an interrelated whole, his medical background would reinforce the tendency to conceptualize society in holistic terms, rather than as the sum of separate phenomena. Distrusting over-specialization, he made a point of attacking the problem even in medicine. He identified it particularly with American influences, and in the 1920s he published an article with the title "American Methods in Medical Education." In it he wrote that

> a new kind of physician and a new kind of surgeon have been developed. The physician studies only a part of the patient; the patient is to him nothing more than a series of microscopic slides or chemical solutions. The surgeon knows the patient merely as an arrangement of typewritten cards. He sees him for the first time unconscious on the table, when he comes like a masked executioner to complete the sentence of the judge.

Among his peers Macphail was probably best known for his remarkable quarterly, *The University Magazine*, which flourished from 1907 to 1920. Created, controlled, and financed by him, it set a standard of excellence and also attained the remarkable circulation of nearly 6,000, which no comparable Canadian quarterly has ever matched. Uncommonly persuasive as an editor, Macphail was able to handle writers, always a prickly lot, with great tact, skill, and firmness. His magazine was notable for paying contributors; in Macphail's mind this was an important principle, for he believed that artists and writers should be remunerated for their work, just as lawyers, physicians, politicians, skilled craftsmen, day labourers, and others expected to be paid. His standard fee for an article was 25 dollars, a sum which was, prior to the First World War, far more than the weekly wage of most people. Because he did pay a fee, he was able to pick and choose from among the best of what was available. In a letter to

MacMechan after the second issue, he stated that "It is not for what I put into the Magazine I take credit, it is for what I kept out. I had a bitter passage with two important personages." If he did not think a submission met his standard, the identity of the author did not deter him from rejecting it, and the fact that he paid for articles meant that he was in a strong moral position to refuse since, when soliciting contributions, he had not asked anybody for charity.

Macphail welcomed purely literary works, but for him the magazine was more than a literary venture. It was also a vehicle to advance a particular ideology that had to do with a Canada that was rural, traditional, and imperial in sentiment. Rural life provided Macphail with a model of what might be called the good society, and represented the affirmative side of his perspective. The traditionalism he supported involved the values associated with rural life, and the political heritage passed down through the ages from Great Britain. The imperialism that he advocated is a difficult concept to translate into the lexicon of the late 20th century. For Macphail - as for Leacock and many other outspoken Canadian imperialists - it did not mean or imply any subordination of Canada to Britain; it meant power-sharing and equality between Canada, the United Kingdom, and the other "white" dominions. It was the opposite of dependency, and indeed Kipling endorsed his writing on imperialism as being "beyond praise ... forasmuch as it dares to indicate that the new countries also have duties."

For the Dominion of Canada as a whole, the period when Macphail began to write on national themes was the best, in terms of growth, that the new country had experienced. After a long economic depression in the late 19th century, at last Canada seemed to be coming into her own, to be a "success." The years prior to the First World War were a period of almost unlimited optimism. Industrialization was accelerating, cities were growing, and the West was being settled by immigrants from many countries. Yet Macphail, like many other intellectuals of the day, believed that the progress of Canadian intellectual and political life was not keeping pace with the country's material development. In fact, where others celebrated economic expansion, Macphail perceived a danger that he would identify explicitly in *The Master's Wife*: "There is no culture when people are engrossed in material things." *The University Magazine* was his highly successful attempt to create a forum for a more elevated calibre of public discussion. He was his own best contributor, with 43 pieces of political comment and social criticism.

At the core of Macphail's social criticism was rejection of urbanism, industrialization, and materialism, all of which he associated with American influences. He insisted on asking contemporary Canadian society "Why?" The following is an example of the sort of writing he produced for *The University Magazine*, drawn from an article entitled "The Dominion and the Spirit," published in 1908. He was focusing on the work of Canadians, and he took as an example the growing of wheat.

It is of some importance that we [Canadians] should make wheat to grow. The thing which is of more importance is that we should have a right reason for undertaking that labour, and a right spirit in the doing of it. The man who makes two blades of wheat to grow where only one grew before, for the mere purpose of providing unnecessary food, is working with the spirit and motive of a servant - of a slave even. The slave works because he is compelled to; the artist because he loves to; the fool does unnecessary work because he is a fool. Each of us is part slave, part artist, and part fool. The wise man is he who strives to be all three in due proportion, and succeeds in being not too much of any one. But the tragedy of our life lies in this: that the man who was designed for an artist is by compulsion so often a slave....

Work, then, in itself is neither good nor bad.... This "work for work's sake" is entirely modern; and our present civilisation is the only one which has ever been established upon that principle. To the Greek mind it was incredible that a free man should labour, even for his own support. That was the business of the slave. The citizen had other occupation, in considering how he could make the best of his life. His business was to think how he should govern himself, how he might attain to a fulness of life.

It is not the modern view that a man should occupy himself with his life. With all our talk about freedom, we have only succeeded in enslaving ourselves. We have created for ourselves a huge treadmill; and, if we do not keep pace, we fall beneath its wheels. Our inventions have only added to the perplexities of life. We have created artificial necessities, and consume our lives in ministering to them.

It is possible to apply this perspective to an analysis of Macphail's own life and activities. He had spent many years working hard as a medical student and as a practising physician. When he had reached a position of financial security, he decided to confine his activities to what he genuinely enjoyed doing: teaching, writing, and editing. He put most of his energy in the pre-war period into writing on current topics in a reflective way - occupying himself with his life.

When the war ended, Macphail was 54 years of age and suffering from glaucoma and other eye problems which made it difficult for him to read. Indeed, for months in 1919 he was not permitted to read. *The University Magazine* was in decline, in part because of his long absence, but also because the post-war world was a different place. The costs associated with the First World War meant that the closer union with Great Britain that Macphail and other Canadian imperialists had sought would not occur; and the war had accelerated the flight from the countryside to the towns. Moreover, in the post-war world the reading public was much more fragmented, and writers themselves tended to be more specialized. The ideal of the man-of-letters, the self-confident generalist, which Macphail had embodied, was dying. After publishing four more issues in 1919-20, he discontinued *The University Magazine*.

During the 1920s Macphail concentrated first on the official history he had been commissioned to write. His other publications during the remainder of his career displayed little of the engagement with contemporary affairs which his work had featured while his causes still seemed hopeful. It was in the late 1920s that he began work on *The Master's Wife*. By 1929 he had described it as finished. He then submitted it to each of his children for judgement, and made changes on the basis of their suggestions. Through the last decade of his life he continued to revise the manuscript, and he appears to have taken more care with this work than with any other; he considered it to be the best book he had written.

The Master's Wife is a work of art, written by a man who was a supreme artist in words. As Pelham Edgar, professor of English literature at Victoria College, Toronto, and like Leacock and MacMechan a long-time member of the editorial committee of *The University Magazine*, wrote at the time of Macphail's death, "his artistic impulse was as strong as his convictions. If a thing was worth saying it was worth saying well." In this book Macphail was saying the most important things of all: about himself, his parents, his social environment, his cultural heritage, and his beliefs. It may be noted that his own position in relation to community values appears ambiguous at some points. He clearly prefers the relatively secular, worldly, and humanistic attitudes of his mother's relatives to the strong sabbatarianism and intense earnestness of his father. Moreover, he and the other children had no doubt that their own place was not on the farm. Commenting on the sometimes-harsh domination of life by the elemental force of nature, he wrote: "Of one thing we were all convinced from the first: we would escape from the land and the ice." Thus although he would eventually base his social criticism on his affection for the local way of life, and especially the farming component of it, and his hostility to all which undermined it, he himself had taken the first opportunity to escape from it. Perhaps this is an example of what he describes as "that fatal capacity to see the paradox of things, that is, both sides of a subject at the same time."

It should be emphasized that in addition to this personal aspect, the way of life portrayed in *The Master's Wife* was crucial for the intellectual formation of Macphail. Leacock once remarked that underneath all of Macphail's half-bantering talk in the University Club of Montreal about rural life, especially the rural life he had known as a boy, "was a deep-seated feeling that the real virtue of a nation is bred in the country, that the city is an unnatural product." He believed strongly that the largely self-sufficient farming which he had known in Orwell, with its independence, dignity, approximate equality, and virtual absence of poverty, was the ideal basis for society. He was critical of western Canadian farming, with its single-crop production, its high levels of investment in machinery, and its dependence upon (and consequent vulnerability to) the international market for the single crop. It was too much like an industry transplanted into the countryside. But the "mixed" family farm, producing to meet most of the needs of its own members, meant that farmers and their families were largely independent of international markets and of the marketplace in general. People were valued as people, not as factors of production. This was the way of life that provided him with the basis for his social criticism, with its steadfast opposition to the industrialization and urbanization of Canada. A semi-autobiography, a document in Canada's social history, a statement of a social and political philosophy, and beautifully written, *The Master's Wife* is a book of rare richness.

Macphail published fragments of the manuscript in the form of short stories, personal reminiscences, and even brief dramas. His recollections of "The Old School" (Orwell), "The Old College" (Prince of Wales), and "The Old University" (McGill) were delivered over national radio. But he did not live to publish the entire manuscript as a book. He died in 1938, and it did not appear in print until late the following year. *The Master's Wife* was brought into the world with a double disability: it was launched shortly after the start of a world war which preoccupied public attention, and its author had died a year earlier. By the time the war was over, the book was "old news" - six years old - and Macphail had been dead seven years. In fact, there was a third problem. His two children published *The Master's Wife* through a private arrangement with a printer. The result was an aesthetic success: a handsome volume with a fine selection of photographs of leading characters, there is no doubt that Macphail would have been proud of it. But the method, with its lack of linkage to a system of distribution, combined with the circumstances of 1939 to bury the book in terms of public consciousness. Over the next several decades, one of the few writers to give it extended treatment was Edgar, who in 1947 made it a major focus of much of an article on his friend Macphail in the *Queen's Quarterly*.

The book became a sort of hidden treasure in Canadian literature. Although I was born, raised, and educated in Prince Edward Island, I myself first learned of it as an undergraduate at McGill in the Honours programme in History. A student in that programme had to attach himself to an individual professor for the final two years; and, as one of his five courses in each of those years, the student worked on a two-year research project under the direction of that professor. I met my professor once every two weeks to discuss progress, and sometimes the conversation wandered from my topic, which was the foundation and early history of Ontario Hydro. Somehow, Macphail's name came up, probably because the professor knew I was from Prince Edward Island. Yet aside from the location of Macphail's home in Orwell, I knew little about him. So his name arose in part because my professor, John Irwin Cooper, had been at McGill long enough to remember him from the 1930s, first as a student and then as a professor. A specialist in the history of Quebec with an encyclopedic knowledge of Canadian history in general, he recommended *The Master's Wife* as the best memoir or book of any kind on the post-pioneering generation in rural Canada in the 19th century. I sought out the book that same day in the stacks of the university library. Once I picked it up, I could not put it down, and I read it through once. The next day I came back and read it a second time.

In 1977 a national publishing house, McClelland and Stewart, produced a paperback edition of *The Master's Wife* for its prestigious New Canadian Library series, with a brief introduction by myself. This provided national distribution for the book, which had long been available only through shops specializing in rare books and some libraries. At last it began to receive the circulation and recognition it merited. For example, ten years after the reprint of *The Master's Wife*, Canadian writer Janice Kulyk Keefer published a landmark book of literary criticism concerning Maritime writing, *Under Eastern Eyes*. In that volume, focusing on the way Macphail revealed the Orwell of his youth through the mind of a child, she praises "the peculiar honesty and almost total absence of nostalgia" in the book. His method, combining childlike perceptions "with the mobility which adult experience and understanding permit... permits us a perfectly dual vision - we see the people of Orwell as they saw themselves, and as they were there to be seen." Kulyk Keefer highlights the book's transcendence of convention, and entirely because of *The Master's Wife*, she ranks Macphail with such major Maritime writers as Thomas McCulloch, T. C. Haliburton, and Joseph Howe. With its power, its rich texture, and its complexity, the book is, in her view, "one of the finest and oddest pieces of prose to be found in Maritime, or Canadian literature as a whole."

Kulyk Keefer has not been alone in marvelling at the special nature of Macphail's achievement. Bumsted, four years earlier in *The Oxford Companion to Canadian Literature*, characterizes *The Master's Wife* as "*sui generis*" for its blend of autobiographical memoir, history, and novelistic technique, and notes that the book's defiance of neat categorization as either literature or history has been a factor which has led to its being unjustly neglected. Writing in 1985, Kenneth MacKinnon, a professor of English at Saint Mary's University in Halifax, places the author in the Gaelic tradition. "The traditional chronicler in Gaelic has to perform a variety of allied literary, scholarly, historical, and genealogical functions. Macphail manages these separate roles with surprising insight and great economy of expression." It is fitting that Macphail, the brilliant stylist and arch-critic of modern life, should wed originality in technique with a deeply traditional combination of roles. This overdue scholarly attention has come because the book is now accessible, for it is clear from references in the work of Kulyk Keefer and others that they have relied on the 1977 reprint.

Since the 1970s there has been a renewed appreciation of Macphail in Prince Edward Island. During the summer of 1975 I delivered a lecture on "Sir Andrew Macphail and Orwell" to a full house in the grammar school in Uigg that he had attended almost a century earlier; it was based on a doctoral dissertation on Macphail as a social critic that I had completed for the University of Toronto in the previous year. The lecture was published as the lead article in the inaugural Fall-Winter 1976 number of a new semi-annual periodical, *The Island Magazine,* and over the next 12 years that issue sold more than 7,000 copies. In 1976, the Caledonian Society of Prince Edward Island released a vinyl recording entitled *"Island Scotch…": A Medley from the Scottish Tradition in Prince Edward Island,* consisting of musical selections linked by the Rev Donald A. Campbell reading excerpts from *The Master's Wife.* The album cover describes the book as a "classic account of early Scottish family and community life in Prince Edward Island."

But as knowledge of Macphail's achievements grew, the public also became aware of a problem. Macphail's family had given his property in Orwell to the provincial government in 1961, in the expectation that it would be used as a park for the benefit of the public. Unfortunately, the government did little to maintain it over the succeeding decades. By the late 1980s, the park was no longer in use, the house was in an advanced state of dilapidation, and there were fears that it would not remain standing for long. Vandals even set a fire inside the house.

What followed can only be described as an inspired and inspiring example of "people power." Interested persons from different parts of Prince Edward Island, including some summer residents, expressed publicly their serious concern over the failure to maintain the property. In the course of doing so, they highlighted the importance of Macphail in Island history as well as the inherent beauty of the site. They organized an informal group known as "Friends of Macphail" to raise public awareness of Macphail and his achievements, and to pressure the government into making a commitment to save the house and to keep the property intact. In the spring of 1989, during an election campaign, the government promised to take action. Since then, the Friends have established the "Sir Andrew Macphail (of Orwell, P. E. I.) Foundation Inc." (incorporated 1990), a non-profit charitable foundation, and, using money from both provincial and federal government sources and private donations, have restored the house beautifully. By 1993 they had it fully open to the public. The homestead operates a small conference centre, caters to private groups, and holds fund-raising events. Plans for the future include public lectures and activities reflecting Macphail's own interests. The farm property surrounding the house now features three nature trails, a wildlife nursery, and an ecological forestry project; the on-site interpretation presents Macphail as a prophet of sustainable land use. All this has resulted from an exceptional community effort which overcame official indifference. The commitment was rooted in recognition of Macphail's significance in defining a distinctive Prince Edward Island identity which places value on the non-material aspects of life.

The recognition has continued to grow. In 1992 the *Canadian Medical Association Journal* reprinted the initial Macphail editorial, "Style in Medical Writing." On 26 June 1994 the Historic Sites and Monuments Board of Canada unveiled a plaque in Macphail's honour at the homestead; it had originally, in 1955, been placed at Prince of Wales College. Appropriately, there is now a matching plaque in Gaelic, provided by the Macphail Foundation.

The current volume is a facsimile edition of the original hardbound book which appeared in 1939. Like the restored

Macphail homestead, this edition is a tribute to a man who, with Lucy Maud Montgomery and Milton Acorn, ranks at the summit among writers rooted in Prince Edward Island. This facsimile edition means that this masterpiece set on the Island will at last have broad distribution in its original format. The text itself is testimony to a full life and evidence that the author never lost sight of who he was, the forces that had shaped him, and where he had come from. *The Master's Wife* is a tribute to his people and his place in their time.

Ian Ross Robertson
September 1994

Ian Ross Robertson is Associate Professor of History at Scarborough College, University of Toronto. His research interests focus on Atlantic Canada and Canadian Intellectual History. Most of his recent publications concern the Prince Edward Island land question in the 19th century. He is preparing a book-length study of Sir Andrew Macphail.

THE MASTER'S WIFE

I

IN THE BEGINNING

HE was master of the school : she was the Master's Wife. He was my father : she was my mother. Happy the man, says Ronsard, *qu'une même maison a vu jeune et vieillard.* It is of that house and place, in which I was born, in which I still live, and of those who dwelt therein, that I propose to write, with such skill in the use of words as I first began to learn in it, and have ever since striven to perfect. The remembrance of any life, rich and fresh, should not be lost to the world.

The house and place was Orwell, in Prince Edward Island, correctly known as the garden of the Gulf of St. Lawrence, a world at the time as new as that primeval garden in which other two parents were first blessed, and then faced with the sudden problem of extracting their living from the soil.

The Master and his wife had seen immigrant families who lived in caves of the earth, in shelters built of logs, in houses sawn from the forest by their own hands, and finally in commodious dwellings; but she lived to see one of those houses grow into a place suitable for a table whereon the proper complement of wine glasses might be displayed at one time for the refreshment of important persons. Between these two extremes the whole course of civilization flowed. The history of that old house is the history of man; it is contained within the period of a hundred years. The house may well be called old, for in it five successive generations of one family have found shelter.

The Master's wife was commonly described as a "Smith woman," that is a foreign person whose native place was some miles away. She disliked the designation, as he had the whimsical habit of attributing any peculiarity of conduct in his children to their maternal ancestry. Loud talk, dubious words, inaccessibility or disdain of religious ideas, hardness of heart, pugnacity, a precocious fondness for tobacco or alcohol found that ready explanation. Heredity might be accepted as a fact : it never was allowed to serve as an excuse. Infantile misconduct was merely an aggravation of the sin of Adam, and so liable to the paternal displeasure as well as to the divine wrath. In the mind of the child these two consequences were one and inseparable; he always considered "Adam" to be the generic name of his mother's people.

And yet even a child was quick enough to discover this rift in the family discipline. We were a family of ten, and ten children in a moderate house must be kept under a strict control if life is to be at all tolerable. The discovery came in a simple way. Her uncle was a sea-captain by a brevet conferred by himself. At the conclusion of every voyage he would come to see us. He rode upon a horse, as the journey was one of five miles through the woods, across the source of streams. He always brought some small presents, a piece of silk, a box of spice, a parcel of strange green tea, a white loaf of sugar, a bottle of French brandy.

His coming was such a tremendous event that the Master found himself quite powerless. Indeed, he could not conceal his own interest and pleasure in the prospect of a breath of intelligence from the larger world. The sea-captain rode solidly, and there were plenty heralds of his approach. As he came up the garden he addressed the Master as William, his wife as Catherine, in a voice as if he were hailing a man in the top. The children were rather embarrassed being witness to the familiarity of his address to persons so august. When he came within, and had distributed his gifts, he called for glasses, and produced his bottle. She understood the ritual, as if she were assisting at a rite which she had long since learned; and we began to suspect a world of experience before our arrival upon the scene.

With his powerful hairy hands the captain sent the tongs crashing through the sugar-loaf, until the whole glistening fabric lay in white lumps upon the table. For the adults he poured hot water in the glass, dropped in a lump of sugar, and filled it up with brandy. He put neither water nor sugar in his own. For the children he put the remainder of the sugar in small glasses until they were full. Then he saturated the sugar with brandy, and handed a glass to each from the eldest to the youngest. The Master sipped his drink with a restraint which was not quite sincere; his wife set her portion in the cupboard against a more leisured moment; the grandmother drank freely, and her eyes shone. The taste of that sugared brandy was delicious in the mouth, and more than one child framed the vow that some day they should have a bottle of their own. They have kept that youthful vow.

When the time came for the sea-captain to leave, he put the remnant of the bottle in his saddle-bag, with a word of apology for his parsimony, "I shall be calling at Nancy's."

" And you will tell her we are all well, " the mother charged him.

"Yes, and that they are good children, " he said as he scrambled upon his horse. The Master winced under the concession; the mother smiled at the approval.

"Good children," he repeated. "And I will tell her too," he added in his loud chanting voice from the top of his horse, "a man might be amongst them for a week, and not hear as much as 'God damn your soul.'" It was not long before one of the children employed this form of words deliberately and publicly, and when put to the question, quoted his uncle as his authority. The defence was a complete success. He was well aware that his mother would not allow the custom of her family to be impugned beyond a certain point. But he did not repeat the experiment.

It was from this uncle we first learned that there were strange themes in the world, fresh words, and new rhythms, hitherto undiscovered in catechism, Bible, or prayer. He talked of ships and the sea. On his last voyage, during a storm a Russian wished to have a reckoning of his position. The incident was amazing. This man who now sat quietly in that retired house had been in a ship-at-sea in a storm. He had encountered a Russian, or a "Rooshian," as he called him to our secret amusement; and the Russian was compelled to avail himself of an intelligence superior to his own.

But the sound and savour of his words instructed us even more than the narrative : the Russian was a barque; he ran down the wind; he came up under my stern — an immodest word to use in presence of the Master. He hailed me and asked for his position. He could not hear; I took my speaking trumpet; yet he could not hear against the wind — unshipped my cabin door — wrote with a piece of chalk — slung the door to the starboard mizzen shrouds. He lifted his spy-glass; bowed to the deck; and squared away.

II

THE SPAR MAKER

THE Master's wife was the daughter of a spar-maker. To make a spar in the craft of ship-building is like making a sonnet in the craft of letters. He moved from place to place where a ship was being built and ready for her spars. A spar-maker works alone as a poet does. He would set up his benches in a retired grove apart from the yard; he would eat and sleep by himself. His work took him as far as the Miramichi. In that strange place his custom was not known, nor his reticence, as he thought, sufficiently respected. A sailor was incautious. He struck the man with his fist and killed him. The Smiths were a passionate people.

That is the account given to us by his own first cousin, but this cousin was always considered a boaster. We often asked the mother for the truth of the matter, but she evaded a denial. She always disliked the categorical answer. She too wished her family to be thought well of. She did add, however, that her father was a tall straight man with a brown flowing beard; and she had heard that his forearm was as thick as another man's thigh. The utmost she would admit was that if he had struck the sailor he would have killed him, and "it served him right."

In later years we often discovered that she had old and secret wishes which we did our best to satisfy. One of the things she "longed for all her life" was to have a suitable stone erected at her father's grave. At a time when the old family property was "passing to strangers," she had the design to make that claim, but she concluded it would be just as well to "let the tail go with the hide," and nothing was done.

I went to the man in Montreal who usually supplied me with grave-stones, ordered a proper monument of granite, and wrote for him the necessary inscription. As he put on his spectacles to read, he said, "I suppose you are in a hurry for this." When he observed that the date of the death was 1854, he added, "The man has been without a stone for sixty years, and I suppose a week or two either way does not matter."

In due course the stone arrived, and a day was set apart for its erection. We drove to the cemetery, six miles away — the mother and three of those children, now themselves grown old. Whilst the men were at work, we lit a fire and made tea. We had luncheon in the open. Then she led us about the cemetery, and using each stone as a theme instructed us in biographies that went back a hundred years. She showed us one of fine slate, with the top gently curved, and the apex polished smooth. Sixty years before, she had seen the Minister McLennan sharpen his razor upon that surface preparatory to his Sabbath morning ceremonial. She showed us the first stone ever erected. It bore the name MacMillan. This man was hewing a sill for the original church, and wondered who would be the first to be buried in the fresh grave-yard. He himself was.

The monument that aroused her deepest interest was one erected to the memory of a woman who was described upon it as "daughter of the Earl of Selkirk." She admitted that she knew the woman, "when she was a young girl," and added, "She used to eat opium, and would walk to the town twenty miles on the ice for the drug, scattering salt before her as she came to a slippery place." There were no rubbers in those days. Here was an old tragedy. She would say no more. "But it is on the monument," we pressed. "You cannot believe all you see on a monument," she said. "You will be putting things on my own that none of yourselves will believe." But the in-scription to the Earl's daughter is there to this day in the Belfast church-yard, which is now the name misapplied to that lovely region known to the earlier French settlers as Belle-Face.

Her father had taken to wife Margaret Moore. Some said she was part English; others said she was part Methodist. It may have been so. That would account for her own extreme toleration. On several occasions one heard her admit that she had known "many good people among the Methodists." Indeed there was a further traditional ancestress, Margaret Mayne, "a red haired woman, the most beautiful ever came out of Ireland." In her hypothetical de-scendants there is more trace of the redness than of the beauty. The legend may therefore be half true.

The Moores lived, and still live, on the rich land that slopes down from Tea Hill to Pownal Bay. There is yet the remains of an old ship-yard at the shore, and it is easy to surmise how the tall straight powerful spar-maker with the flowing brown beard found a wife.

Moores of the third and fourth generation yet live in that old place. It lies on the way from Orwell to the town. We often pass it by, but rarely enter, as the ceremonial of a call would occupy two days at least. At times and in various places one meets the elder occupant, and there is a sudden gush of affection.

The spar-maker died, and left a family of young children, two sons and four daughters. He had no foothold in the land; he followed where ships were built. His children were scattered. Two sons and their mother went to Georgetown to the house of an uncle whose name was John. He was known as "Major," for no better reason than his rank in a regiment of militia. According to the account given by the Master's wife, he was a merchant; but we always suspected that the commodity he traded in was rum. Certainly, at Christmas time he would spend the day at his old home, a distance of fifteen miles, and would bring for the event a small keg beautifully made, and bound with hoops of brass.

But she always defined occupations in the light of her own predilections. If she liked the man, a pedlar was a commercial traveller; a money lender was a banker; a politician was a statesman. Other-

wise, a man who lent money was a usurer, and the
merchant an oppressor of the poor. In like manner,
an idiot was merely innocent, backward or dull. Her
diagnosis of the various stages of insanity was quite
definite. In the case of a person she liked, the woman
was at first depressed, then discouraged, then melancholy. When the husband's mother or sisters talked of putting her to the asylum, the poor creature
would lose her mind completely, as a result of such
inconsiderate talk. In other cases the condition was
due to heredity. There had been one original family
in the place with a marked taint of insanity. The
malady would break out in the most unexpected
persons, but a relationship could always be traced to
that family, no matter what name the sufferer might
bear. The history was quite clear for five generations,
and she had a peculiar gift in tracing it to the original
source; possibly in certain cases with an element of
satisfaction.

This uncle of hers was otherwise dubious apart
from his occupation. He had an illegitimate son.
There was no secret about it. The boy's name,
contrary to custom, appears on his father's monument, although with proper reticence the mother's
name is not given. This young man attained to the
status of a school teacher. He was paralysed on the
left side and in the right eye; but he wrote an excellent
script. He made some pretension to scholarship, and
was in the habit of using the Latin — incorrectly, as
one may yet observe, when he was called upon to

inscribe a sentiment in an autograph album. Not that she ever held this lapse against her uncle. Indeed, in later years for economic reasons she lamented the decay of illegitimacy. "In my time," she would say, "there used to be plenty of them; but now the young women in that condition go to the States, and both mother and child are lost as servants in the settlement."

The fate of children in an alien home is uniformly pathetic. One of these two boys, her brothers, came to see us sixty years after he had left his uncle's house. He was a tall fair man, not yet frail, and with an unquenchable curiosity. He carried a two-foot rule, and was discovered making careful measurements of the house at Orwell. He announced with as much enthusiasm as if he had just succeeded in measuring the solar universe, that the house was 56 feet across the front and 107 feet "from stem to stern." This statement like many an other, though true in itself, was quite inadequate, as it gave no account of the height or form of the fabric. To him a house was the work of one's own unaided hands. This feat in mensuration provided him with a subject of wonder for the rest of his days.

He was a correct man; he wore the ceremonial clothes of black with a white shirt unstarched; he was in some distress as he had lost his "satchel" on the way. His sister had the shirt washed for him surreptitiously, as she thought, whilst he lay in his bed. But she always lived under the illusion that

nothing was seen which she did not wish to be seen,
nothing heard that she wished to be secret. She herself never believed anything she did not wish to believe. Her account of any event was the best that
could be made, and for her it was the truth. That
was the source of her courage and her strength. To
the Master, this was mere pride, a false or fierce pride;
but he never succeeded in breaking that spirit.

The time came when these two boys, her brothers, were to go out of their uncle's house, and their
mother went with them. There was free land "to
the westward." They loaded their belongings upon
a cart. The journey was ninety miles. The place was
Egmont Bay, and the land had all the disabilities
that free land usually has. After sixty years the
remembrance of that journey was quite fresh in his
mind, and he spent a long summer afternoon in
recalling it. But it was the strangeness and humour
of the adventure that he remembered best. The worst
thing about it was that he had to drive back the cart,
and return on foot the distance of ninety miles. The
uncle gave them nothing for a beginning in their new
world, "not so much as a chalk-line and black-stick."
The truth is that, although he was a "merchant," he
had nothing to give.

To build a house in those days was a simple affair.
The tools required for a beginning were a chalk-line
and black-stick, a narrow ax, a broad-ax and a whip-
saw. A tree was felled, trimmed of branches, and
cut to proper length. A strip of the bark was re-

moved. The line was fixed by a brad-awl or nail at one end. It was blackened by passing it over a black-stick, which was a piece of alder-wood charred in the fire. Then the line was drawn taut along the white strip, lifted in the middle, and let go. A black line was left, by which the log could be hewn to a flat surface. With his ax the workman bit into the log to the line at intervals of a foot. With his broad-ax, which has a short handle set off from the blade for greater freedom, he slashed off the sections between the cuts at a single stroke. The log was turned on the flat, and the process repeated until a squared timber was secured.

Sills, posts, plates, rafters, joists, studs, were hewn from trees of corresponding size. The boards were ripped from the largest logs. A pit like a long grave was dug and skids were laid across. The log was rolled on these. One boy would enter the pit; the other would stand upon the timber, and with a two-handled saw they would rip off the boards, the top-sawyer guiding the cut, the bottom-sawyer doing most of the work. For shingles the log was sawn across in short lengths. The block was split with a wide iron wedge; the pieces were thinned at the end with a draw-knife, and the edges made true with a jack-plane. When the lumber was assembled the building of the house was a mere diversion, and the boys learn-ed their trade as the work progressed. To build a framed house was a long labour, and these two young pioneers with their mother were, like their neighbours, content for some years with a house built of unhewn logs; but this is not a book on architecture.

This old man had come to Orwell when he was quite young, although at the time he seemed to be of mature age. One summer morning he and his brother came in a light wagon to the Master's house. They were dressed in black, their faces severely grave.

"How is mother?" the Master's wife enquired.

"She is well," the elder of the two replied, and after a suitable pause added the fatal words:

"I trust."

The import of his message was apparent to all, for that was the formula in which death was announced. She expressed no emotion. She never did. Forty years afterwards, when it was announced to her by night that the Master was dead, hearing the message, all she said was "Dear, dear," and arose from her bed, alert for the new duties inseparable from the event. She was never known to shed a tear. I was sixteen years old before I saw a grown woman cry. I thought it a degrading spectacle.

The two young men had come a little in advance. The procession of wagons appeared over the crest of the hill, and soon entered the garden. The coffin was borne on an "express," a four-wheeled vehicle well sprung but without seats. The distance travelled was eighty miles, and the journey had occupied two days. The horses were driven at a trot, and the innovation was excused on the ground of necessity. Relatives on the route joined, and the funeral procession was now grown to an imposing length. The coffin was opened in the garden, and for the first time we looked death in the face. After a meal the mourners continued on their way six miles further, and "little Mamma" was buried by the side of her husband, the spar-maker, in Belle-Face.

III

HER PEOPLE

THE earliest printed reference to the settlement of
these Smiths in Canada is contained in a book by
Walter Johnstone entitled, *Travels in Prince Edward
Island.* As a perfect work of history, this book des-
erves a place with Caesar's *Commentaries* and the
writings of George Borrow. It contains not one mean
word, not one imperfect sentence. A copy was sent
to me, probably in jest, by Walter Gow from Toronto,
at one time deputy-minister in London. He was a
cousin of John McCrae, and supplied me with much
material when I was editing *In Flanders Fields,* a
collection of the poems and letters, with a biography,
of the dead poet, a labour of love undertaken for his
mother. This book of travel is extremely rare; it is
also expensive, as the many persons to whom it was
lent, in trying to secure a copy for themselves, have
bid up the price. Once in a railway train, I observed
a man reading the original copy, but I have not seen
it since.

Walter Johnstone, who wrote in the year 1821, in
deploring the lack of books on the Island, relates that
he came into the house of a gentleman from Perthshire, who had a Gaelic Bible. This was the "original
Smith settler." His first name was Alexander; he

too is buried at Belle-Face. His native place was in the northern part of Perthshire amongst the Highland foothills. In the year 1798 with his family he left his home on the great American migration. He must have been a considerable person, for he paid thirty guineas for each passage. The place of departure was Portree. The day before sailing he sent all his goods on board, and with his family slept ashore. In the night the ship vanished and left him stranded, without money, without any earthly thing. It was three years before he recovered strength for a fresh adventure, and it was 1802 before he reached the Island.

This pioneer was capable of great and sudden effort, but he was easily discouraged in the labour of clearing the land. With a club in his hand, he killed a bear that had broken into his farmyard; but his wife must pretend to assist him in the more arduous work of piling and burning logs. About this woman there are two legends : that she had been companion to a "titled lady"; that she, herself, was the titled one. In all immigrant societies these legends are common: sometimes they are true.

He took land in the woods at the head of tidewater where a fresh stream fell in. The place was known as Newton. In time he had six sons and three daughters. Their fate would be long to trace in detail. Some married, and settled. One of them was father of the Master's wife. In the end two sons, William and James, and a daughter, Nancy, remained all unmarried; and they died one by one. It was by these three on the old place that the Master's wife was adopted as a child when her father died. Their land was good. It yielded an easy living. They were not poor. They had inherited all there was; they had no children to goad them into expense, and land them in debt.

A man who lives on his own land and owes no man anything develops all the dignity inherent in his nature. These three lived a dignified and abundant life, and kept themselves vainly aloof from the later immigration. They were from the "mainland." The new arrivals were from the Isle of Skye. The Gaelic word for a native of Skye is *Sgiathanach*. They now call themselves Hebrideans. The term is merely descriptive of one who comes from the "winged isle," but in time this fine word acquired a suggestion of separateness, and when used with malice, a tinge of reproach. It was never heard in the Master's house. The use of that term was mortal sin; it signified the sin of pride, and as there was no open sin in the family he was alert for sins of the heart. But the Smiths used the term boldly. When the last survivor was old and fallen on evil times, he brought a nephew into the house with the design of making him the inheritor. But when the young nephew began keeping company with the perfectly proper daughter of a neighbour, whose ancestor had come from Skye, he would not allow it. "Was I going to have a *Sgiathanach* in my own corner ? " he asked absurdly, in justice to himself. These notions had no place in the new world.

In that well ordered house the young Catherine learned all the craft of housewifery, which in those days was something more than asking the cook what she would suggest for dinner. These people had brought with them from Scotland the best practice of farm life. Nearly all that was used in the house was made in the house, and every art and industry must be learned. This involved a knowledge of animals and their products, of fruits, vegetables, and grains. It was not enough to make butter and cheese; the cow and her calf must be learned. Before the sheep was shorn the lamb must be reared. The wool was to be washed at the stream in water warmed in an iron pot over an open fire; dried in the sun; picked free of chaff, burrs, and seeds; carded, spun, and woven into cloth light enough for a woman's dress, heavy enough for blankets or great-coat for a man. The cloth itself after it left the loom must be scoured, thickened, combed, and dressed under hot irons.

Nor was this all. The white wool and the black wool made white or black cloth; white warp and black woof made various patterns; blended white and black made grey. With cotton warp a lighter fabric for women and children was woven. Warp dyed with indigo could be bought, but all other colours were made in the house. The dyes were found in the woods — oak and hemlock-bark for browns, various species of lichens known as *crotals* or *crottles* for other shades. Combined with copperas these materials produced colours from green to inky black.

The utmost the men of that house could do was

to kill and dress the animals for food; the details of salting, smoking, and spicing were left to the women. They gained all skill in *charcuterie* — puddings white and brown, tripe, sweet-breads, hearts, liver, calves-head, known contemptuously to the English as "offal." During the War the English starved themselves on scanty meat, whilst the aliens amongst them lived luxuriously upon these despised dainties. The killing of the animals in the early winter had all the solemnity of a sacrificial rite, and amongst the Smiths it was performed with full pomp. As a very young child I happened upon the scene in company with the Master. The five tall brothers were standing in a row, contemplating with sorrow their sad but necessary task — two beeves, four pigs, two sheep, and a heifer, hanging in a red but cleanly line above a litter of bright straw to conceal the gruesome and bloody snow.

These animals for years had been loving friends, and now they made a cheerful sacrifice for human need. It sometimes happened that an animal was spared from year to year by reason of the affection it inspired or admiration of its immense size. One such pig grew so heavy it could not stand; it finally "dressed" 642 pounds. After due contemplation and comment, the procession moved into the house, and completed the ceremony with a bottle of Barbados rum. On similar occasions at his own place the Master would complete with family worship, in which those who had assisted took part, as if in expiation for the death of those trusting fellow creatures.

I once asked a German prisoner, as part of my duty, if he had enough food. "Enough, but not plenty," he said. That was the situation in this house where the Master's wife was brought up. The food must be wrought for and arranged in advance. One year the flour gave out before the new harvest arrived. The wheat was always reaped with sickles, as it still is in Belgium. She took a sheaf from the field, scorched off the chaff in the fire, beat out the grain, ground it in a hand mill, sifted the flour, and had bread baked when the reapers returned.

The custom was to take the wheat to the mill in the winter, on the ice along the shore and across the rivers. In that year of early need her uncle put a bag of four bushels on the back of a horse, and walked alongside, through the woods by the head of the rivers, to the mill, a distance of twenty-seven miles. He returned the next night with the flour. The Master's wife often told us that the taste of that bread never left her mouth.

The Smiths limited their desires within the range of the work they desired to do : they never allowed their desires to impose work upon them. They had all those Highland eccentricities so faithfully chronicled by Stuart of Garth; they were equally void of the two chief curses of mankind, luxury and ambition; they were possessed of a proud indolence and held themselves superior to want. They worked with such care that they got little done, and finished nothing. They built themselves a comfortable solid warm house; but they never finished all the rooms inside. The walls were of thick pine planks, halved or rebated, like the hull of a ship. Some of the rooms were properly plastered; some were merely lathed; but the vast "other end" showed the smooth planks; and the upper storey was an open loft filled with treasures — tools, lumber, saddles, chests, and the spoil of ships wrecked upon the coast. In one room under a bed was a gravestone properly inscribed, which they never had the energy or leisure to erect in its final place.

Their land was good and its virgin soil not yet exhausted. Many pine trees remained, and they were easily converted into money. When one of these old men at last found that he had need of a doctor, he cut down one of the pine trees, hauled it to the mill which was now near at hand, had it sawn into boards, and sold them for thirty dollars. He went to the town by the steamer, but it was well understood that resort to a doctor was merely part of the ceremonial of dying. This doctor was an honest man. His son and his son's son yet practice medicine in that same town. He advised his patient to go home "and save his few coppers." Another sign of bad omen was a negro on a ship that came in that day from the West Indies. He had never seen a "black man" before. To describe this portent was the chief interest of his few remaining days, and he spoke with great conviction, as if he expected no one to believe him.

It was not unusual in those days for people to stay at home. Many persons never reached as far as the town. Dugald Bell from the South Shore, being a rare visitor, was eighty-seven years old before he saw an organ-grinder and a monkey, although he was a rich man. He gazed upon the creature and reflected, "Old age will come to any man." The monkey went about, and having gathered the coppers in his cap, thrust them in his mouth. The observer remarked, with fellow feeling for another careful veteran, "The little fellow is very fond of the money, whatever."

The Master's wife found something unseemly in her uncle's consternation over the negro, and protested that "the man was as God made him." With her intense human sympathy, her passion for all who were oppressed, her devotion to those who were kind, with her inability to believe anything contrary to her desire, she had two explanations of the negro : either he was not a negro, or he could be white if he preferred that colour. After one of her rare journeys by railway, she was asked if the people had been good to her. She selected one for special praise. He would place a pillow, fetch tea, and carry her bag; but she was elaborately vague about his identity. We surmised that this paragon was the coloured porter on the train, and asked her if he was a black man.

"His mother might have been a dark woman" was the utmost of her admission; and yet she always prided herself upon her extreme truthfulness.

To her uncles' family came the inevitable end. There were no children in the house, and a farm cannot be managed without children. They would not yield to new methods. The open fireplace, the scythe, the sickle, the flail, the gig remained with them long after the appointed time. They would not work. When visitors came, all operations were at an end. In the busiest season they would desert the field and sit by the fire to entertain and be entertained. Even the women who were preparing the meal were not allowed to disturb the entertainment. If they wished access from one side of the stove to the other, they were compelled to pass behind the half circle of chairs. Their sister, Nancy, was now grown bent and aged, but her obscure grumbling was kept under control by fear of their violent reproaches if they were disturbed. When all were dead but one, he sold the place for four thousand dollars. He wasted the money, and in the end sought refuge in the house of a nephew, where he soon died. The nephew himself at the time was a man of seventy, the last of the breed, massive, grave, handsome, kind, but with a deep passionate voice. He recited the tragedy. When he reached the climax, he arose with a deliberate dramatic emphasis, crossed the room to the fireplace, and brought back a chip of wood, which he had selected after just appraisement.

"When the old man came to me," he said, holding out the chip, "he had not the value of that."

The Smiths were a peculiar people; they even had a characteristic cough, like the single bark of a fox. It has descended to the fourth generation. They can yet identify one another in the most crowded places. This hereditary gift is not uncommon. I was spending a night with Sir Dawson Williams at St. Omer in a hospital controlled by the Duchess of Sutherland.

She was much concerned about his cough, and had a medicine prepared for him. He took the medicine without demur; but he assured her that he was not very hopeful of the result, as he had the cough since the time of his grandfather at least. By the same sign I once identified a third cousin, a Westaway woman, wife of the premier of the province. All of her children are similarly gifted, but in a very minor degree.

The Smiths, as a family, are long since gone. We still make a pilgrimage to the place, now in the hands of strangers; the house yet standing but put to the uses of a modern farm. In that house we found early kindness, humour, and humanity; a pagan refuge from the problems of sin, of its punishment, and even from the complicated process of the salvation from it.

IV

THE IMMIGRANTS

WILLIAM was the Master's human name. One seldom heard him so addressed. To her children his
wife spoke of him as "your father"; to all else as "the
Master." It was long before we discovered that she
used the term in its specific sense, and that this mastery did not extend to the universe, to the family, or
to herself. In speaking to him there was no need to
use any name. The Highland woman never used her
husband's name; it would be too familiar; she referred
to him as "Himself." The Master's father also was
William, and he was the first of the family to come
to Canada. The year was 1832.

This grandfather has vanished from the earth.
No one now living has seen him. He died seventy-
five years ago. His name is inscribed in Latin upon
the books of King's College, Aberdeen, in the year
1820, where it is also recorded that he was a winner
of a prize for Latin prose. It does not even appear
that he completed his course to graduation. No
picture or letter remains. There is a printed sheet
containing rules for correct handwriting, and it bears
emendations by his son, as if he contemplated a new
edition.

When this grandfather first appeared on the

Island, he was accosted by the minister in the Latin tongue. He passed the test, and they conversed in Latin. That was the sign and seal of his learning, his culture, his birth, and breeding. The Master's wife described him as "a gentleman," a word of which she was chary; but when she used the term all knew what she meant. He had once visited her uncle's house, and as he handed his beaver hat to her, he charged her to put it in a safe place.

He died in the year 1852 at the age of fifty-two, and is buried at Brown's Creek. From that church-yard a bell now rings in his memory, impressed with the words : *VIVOS VOCO MORTUOS PLANGO*. His neighbours at the time were Irish, and a party of them went in advance to dig the grave. The leader was a man named Roche. When he was asked the meaning of this irruption into a Highland settlement, he said that John Murphy, a rival jester, had hanged himself, and they were going to bury him among the Protestants. The funeral was delayed until they had opened the coffin and looked upon the dead man's face.

A strange confirmation of this incident came during a recent year. A grandson, who in turn is named William, practiced the profession of engineer in Oregon. One day an old man, tall and straight, entered his office, and said :

"I just came in to see if you looked like your father — and you do." He told of seeing that funeral halt opposite his father's house seventy-three years ago when he was a child, and he had wondered ever since what was the cause of the delay.

The young scholar left King's College on account of the rising difficulties of the Church of Scotland. The trouble was not religious but financial. The scholarship fund on which he existed became involved. He returned to his home in Nairn, and like many Highland scholars found his living in the school. He married Mary Macpherson of the tribe of Cluny. They went to live at Fort William, some sixty miles to the southward, where he continued his occupation for three years. There is a letter written by his mother to him and his young wife, which is worth printing after the lapse of a hundred years. Her family name was Clark; her husband was James. She wrote with an educated hand, which is all the more remarkable, as few Highland women of the time — or English women either — could write at all. Her letter was written from Nairn under date of 21st December, 1829 :

"To William Macphail, Schoolmaster,
        Cornach, Fort William.

Nairn, December 21st, 1829.

Dear William and Mary :

I received your letter on Thursday, December 15, and was by it happily informed of your good health, and also of Mary's. Your present circumstances afford us no small pleasure, particularly your house, when contrasted with the mean hovel at Glenbanchor, together with the circumstances mentioned, which I think might well call forth the liveliest expression of gratitude from us to God, the giver of all good; and I hope through the grace given you, that you will never enjoy them but in subordination to His will. You remember that when any situation was proposed to you, it was not at all agreeable unless it was a Highland one, which leads me to remark that it was the appointment of Providence; that it was not any casual or common desire you had to be there, but simply this, that it was the will of God it should be so; moreover, how could you and Mary be joined together but in consequence of this taking place; and now it is my earnest prayer and hope you will be so like Zacharias and Elizabeth, walking in all the commandments of the Lord blameless. I am very sorry that you did not come down at the vacation. You promised to come at Christmas but I forbade you, that it might hurry you to come in harvest; and now I am afraid you cannot come owing to the distance and shortness of the day, although I sincerely wish it. I have many things to say which I cannot state at present, particularly to you, my dear Mary. I never had a brother but I loved as a sister and I expect to love you as a daughter. I'm going to give you an advice. Perhaps you know it already, it is this, the more careful you are at first the happier it will be for you through life. I mean domestic affairs, which you must take upon yourself. If you will not keep, he will not, although not a spender; for he is too liberal and has often left himself bare by giving to others, and I hope he will take this advice from you. Do not think I am a miser although I advise you this way. I have not seen your father these 5 weeks and I am timorous as usual. Alexander intends to go and see you although he was prevented from going at the time of your marriage, and I would send the Rug, but it is still awaiting you.

I am, your affectionate mother,

Isabella Macphail."

The comment of the Master's wife upon this letter was that no two persons ever stood in more dire need of advice towards economy, and no two persons ever profited less by it. To them economy was meanness, or a mark of poverty. Late in life, this Mary Macpherson was complaining of the scarcity of sugar in the house.

"Why do you not buy a barrel of it ? "

"Because there is not money enough to buy a barrel."

"Then book it" — that was her remedy. She was not wise in counsel.

"Throw it about their feet," was her solution of every problem. That is what they appear to have done with the school at Fort William. There was however a legend that a powerful man desired the school for a claimant of his own. His name was MacMillan of Cardross, and to the young mind that name signified the "unjust man" of the scriptures, upon whom retribution is promised. The mother also objected to the term "mean hovel," contained in the letter; but that was the designation used by the older woman for any house of which she disapproved.

There was now nothing for the pair but emigration to America. They had two children; the elder of the two was the Master. The destination was Montreal. The voyage lasted nine weeks. Ship-fever broke out. The captain ran for Prince Edward Island, where he knew the Earl of Selkirk had established settlements. A storm arose. The passengers were under closed hatches. Panic broke out. The captain was in despair. Mary, the grandmother, began singing the 46th psalm, and all sang with her :

God is our refuge and our strength,
In straits a present aid :
Therefore, although the earth remove,
We will not be afraid :
Though hills amidst the seas be cast;
Though waters roaring make,
And troubled be; yea, though the hills
By swelling seas do shake.

When Highlanders sing psalms their mood is governed by the psalm they sing, and they can find a psalm to fit every mood. The panic was allayed, and the captain assured the woman that she had succeeded where he had failed. He returned to her a part of the passage money. But the storm increased. The ship was dismasted, and finally cast herself away on the north shore of Nova Scotia close to the mouth of the River John. The passengers and crew escaped with their lives only, save for the few bits that came ashore with the wreckage. This was in the year 1832. How would the newspapers rave over such an event to-day; and yet until this moment there has never been a written or printed word about the disaster.

The castaways were kindly cared for by some American fishermen who were drying their nets and "the shining pieces" of silver they gave to the children were never lost in memory. The immigrant brought ashore in his pocket a copy of *Horace*. It was from that book his grandchildren learned the higher Latin, and it is now in a safe place, still bearing the stain of sea-water. But it was slight equipment for beginning life in a new world, although it was afterwards reinforced, when the tide fell and the wind went down, by a Gaelic Bible and a spinning wheel. These also are yet safe.

In those days shipwreck was a mere incident of travel, an interruption of a journey. His ultimate destination was Napanee, a town beyond Kingston in Ontario, where a cousin of his own was Inspector of Schools. This cousin's name was MacKerras; his son was afterwards professor of classics in Queen's University; his portrait yet hangs in Grant Hall. The distance was near a thousand miles, and the stranger made the journey on foot, along the shores of Nova Scotia, through the forests of New Brunswick, up the St. John River to the St. Lawrence, through Quebec, past Montreal, up Ontario to Napanee.

When he arrived, his cousin was not at home, and the women-kind were strangers to the traveller. He did not even announce himself; he left the house of his kinsman to return to his forlorn family. The women upon reflection surmised there was something unusual in the visitor; they followed him through the woods, and properly invited him to return. He remained for a few days. For some inexplicable reason he did not like Ontario. He walked back the thousand miles of the return journey. He reported on arrival that he had enjoyed his walk immensely, but he left no written word to indicate wherein his enjoyment lay.

The record of the next few years is obscure in remembrance; but his third child was born in Nova Scotia, the following one in Cape Breton, and perhaps

THE MASTER

1860

one other. In those days it was not considered delicate to refer to such events. A child once asked his
mother of the exact house in which she was born, but
he was promptly given to understand that children
had better "attend to their own affairs."

It was the year 1838 before the family arrived in
Prince Edward Island, on the southern shore at
Belle Creek, amongst the Comptons, the Humes, the
Sanders, the Bars. The site of the first house they
occupied, and of the school in which he taught, is yet
shown. A teacher was engaged by a few families, and
it might well be that after a year they would consider
they had extracted from him all the learning that was
good for them. By stages he moved inland, and came
to a final resting place at Upper Newton, about a
mile above the house in which the Smiths lived.
There he died in the year 1852, leaving the Master as
head of the family, he being at the time twenty-one
years of age, and already an elder in the Church of
Scotland.

The family was three sons and four daughters.
One girl and one boy died about this time. The boy's
name was John. He had repute as a scholar and a
wrestler. A collateral descendant was rather a famous wrestler. I went with him to visit the old place,
then in possession of an Irishman named Cody, who
himself in his youth was a wrestler too, and yet had
an eye for form. He scrutinized the stripling boy
with an appraising eye, felt his arms, and then very
modestly asked him "to strip to the waist." When
the symmetry and strength of arms and torso was

revealed to him, he burst out with an invocation to his
Saviour to impose upon him the last retribution, if he
were wrong in his decision that "this boy could throw
his grand-uncle John" — who then had been in his
grave for sixty years. Then with delicate fingers he
examined the intercostal spaces to satisfy himself, as
he surmised, that the ribs were united in a continuous
carapace of bone. He knew that strong men were so
formed on one side at least; but he had never before
seen one who was "solid on both sides."

The Master was faced with the problem of organ-
izing the household. By some kind of authority he
had conferred upon his three sisters and two brothers
the rank of "school-teacher." He himself had inherited the title from his father. There was a sound
scholarship in the family. They had learned the rudiments, that is, reading, writing, arithmetic, unconsciously, as a bird learns to fly. They had a correct
use of language — and they could discover the grammar of it for themselves. Teaching was only required
by those who were intellectually incapable of learning without compulsion, and they were never deliberately taught. The method of learning Latin was
unusual, and not a success. As soon as these children
had the use of letters, they were set to read aloud
from *Horace*, their father's theory being that it was
as easy to learn and understand Latin words as
English words, the letters and sounds being the same.

It might be thought these children were too young
for the dignity of school-teacher, yet the Master had
formally taught school and drew pay in Cape Breton

when he was eight years old; and I myself at the age of twelve drew pay — as a substitute, it is true — for teaching geometry, on the theory that the one-eyed is adequate to lead the blind if the blind are anxious to be led. If not, then there must be a modern school.

There was also the theory that education and the power to teach "ran in families," and these children were welcomed in the schools where their father had once taught. They went far afield, bearing with them the seed of learning, which by generation is fruitful to this day. One of the girls, Mary by name, to secure an engagement, rode fifty miles in one day on a man's saddle, the two stirrups being attached to one side for her use. Even through the woods, where there was no eye to see, she would not "ride in any other way." She would not so much as mention the word "astride." They all came "home" at the end of the week or at the end of the term according to the distance; but the place was "home" to them, long after they had homes of their own.

The Master was left with his mother in the house at Upper Newton. His school was in lower Newton. Twice a day he passed the place where "Catherine" lived. Indeed for a time she had been a pupil in the school. In due course he married her. The ceremonial seems to have been an affair of some pomp. It was fifty years afterwards when I had a full account of it. I was then visiting pathologist to the Hospital for Insane at Verdun near Montreal. One summer afternoon, the superintendent, Dr. T. J. W. Burgess, informed me that he had admitted a patient from my own country, and she had been enquiring for me. He showed me his new patient sitting on a bench under a tree.

In the Master's house was a book entitled, *The Principles of Aesthetics*, which had been presented to him. It was inscribed, "With the hope that it may wile away the ennui of an idle hour." It was one of the first books I had read. I thought the inscription "elegant," and was deeply impressed by the word "ennui." The donor was this same woman; the date 1857, the year before his marriage. She was the daughter of a small dark foreign-looking Englishman who was the country merchant. He had the repute of being a hard man; he "wanted his own"; he had acquired that authority and fear which comes to a man to whom everyone is indebted; it was he who could decide if another man was to have "a handful of hayseed in the spring" for the sowing, or a barrel of flour for his family in the winter. Even the Master's wife had that traditional fear, and now I thought this demented old woman an ironical spectacle. I sat beside her, and she told me some of the things that are written in this book. I had long been familiar with her history. Her father was hard on her; she became depressed, strange, eccentric, melancholy, according to the usual tolerant account. The thing the demented woman remembered best was this marriage; "There was a procession of carriages, and all had ribands on their whips."

V

THE NEW WORLD

THE little house at Newton was filling up again with a new generation. By the year 1864 there were already three children. In the meantime the Master had obtained a grammar school, and walked morning and evening, a distance of more than two miles. This school was between the two headwaters of the Orwell river. The farm upon which the school stood fell vacant. He bought the farm, and moved in on the Queen's Birthday, May 24th, 1864.

James Mavor, that famous geographer and economist, during a visit made the discovery that Prince Edward Island was more than an island, more than a continent even; it was a world in miniature. In a morning drive he traversed lowlands, crossed rivers, passed over watersheds, ascended into highlands, where he viewed bays, harbours, and the ocean itself. On a longer excursion he reached the main summit of the Island, and upon the plateau beheld deserts, lakes, and tundras.

If the traveller pushed on to the north side, he could see in time of storm waves that broke on the reefs and leapt over the lighthouse, to lose their force against the sand-dunes which retreat slowly like divisions of an army striving to protect a front. On

his return to the south side, he would seem by contrast to have come into a sub-tropical region with
its richness and warmth. If he were fortunate, he
would see wrecked ships. In one storm, 135 ships
were cast away, and the bodies of 600 sailors were
washed up on the beach. For many years strangers
would be seen searching for their graves.

Passing down the Orwell River into the bay of the
same name, into Hillsborough Bay, at low tide this
geographer could alight from his canoe by the chan-
nel, and there stand upon the Cambrian formation
with tree-ferns and coal embedded in the rocks. On
either hand would appear a cross section of the geol-
ogical world extending upwards to the newest red
sandstone. If it were an affair of mountains, at times
he could look to the north, and there discover against
the sky ridges, peaks, and pinnacles that could not be
distinguished from cloud masses lit by the evening
sun.

This explorer might even stand within an extinct
crater, from which I, when young and coming in
from the sea, saw fire and smoke and sulphurous
vapours erupt as if it were from a lime-kiln, in such
volume and symmetry as I have not witnessed from
Vesuvius or Etna. This adventurer in that Island
also met with tribes speaking a language he had
never heard, and saw Indians in their wigwams,
making baskets, fish-traps, pottery, bows and arrows,
eel-spears, and nets. He declared his opinion that
a man who travelled from Antwerp to Bagdad would
not see more. Four-and-twenty cement pillars, the

foundations, as some say, of a saw mill destroyed by fire, reminded him of ruined temples in the African or Syriac desert. It was in this world of Orwell we had early being, and the whole universe became familiar to us.

There was also evidence of an earlier civilization; burial places with fragments of stone bearing French names; tools of iron, small, soft, and of unusual shape; and in some localities the French language was yet to be heard. A housemaid, daughter of a neighbour, had a visit from her grandfather. He was upwards of eighty years old, and as his farm was by the sea, he wore a semi-nautical cap. He could spare time for the visit, as his day was already broken. He had spent the morning making snug the grave of his own grandmother in the old French burying-ground, where the first settlers laid their dead before they had established a place of their own.

This old French graveyard, unused for a hundred years, was then a forest with trees twenty inches through. More recently, some neighbours who had arranged to visit it with the design of clearing away the undergrowth, and converting it into a solemn park of remembrance, when they reached the spot discovered that the place had been desecrated. Avaricious persons had cut down the trees for their own use; they put fire to the slash. It was all a blackened area; the stones were reduced to the original sand; a few lettered fragments remained; the very mounds were burned level in the fierce fire.

This old man had been a scholar in the Master's

school, and school-mate of the Master's wife. Having had a drink or two, he continued his round of visits. As I accompanied him to the stile, he said in a mysterious whisper :

"Ask your mother if she ever seen the devil." There was an old and horrid rumour that the devil had arisen from the sea in the guise of a black man, and from afar off pursued a whole company of school girls, until they sought refuge under the eye of the Master. But the company of girls was so large that no inferential turpitude was attached to any one.

"Tell her it was me," the old man continued, with desire to free the community from so invidious a charge. According to the long and gleeful account the impersonator made, it seems that he had stripped himself naked in the woods, and plunged into a hole in the marsh. As the tide rose, at the moment of the skailing of the school, he leaped out, black and glistening with mud, and disported himself in the upper air. When I returned to the house, there was no need to put his question, for the Master's wife remarked.

"He" — this man of eighty — "was a mischievous boy."

The farm was acquired from the Fletchers. The north and south branches of the Orwell River joined within the area, flowed in a deep wooded ravine, passed through the adjoining property, and met the tide where it was crossed by a bridge. Upon this stream were three mills. Heavy timber grew upon either bank. In course of time, the stream and its borders and the land as far as the salt-water fell to us by inheritance or by sale. The stream now runs upon gravel and rock, through grassy meadows where mill-ponds once were, through gorges where with an unerring instinct the early settlers built their three dams, through woods where trees have grown to immense size, protected by the high banks which prevent their removal. There also, as a neighbour observed, "is all the accommodation a sea-trout could require."

The farm was not large, a hundred acres, and there was much waste land. The stream and ravine, and a road that followed it, a brook that fell in, clumps of trees, all occupied space; but the remainder was very good, rich and easily worked. The farm also was a world in miniature. There were upon it horses, cattle, sheep, pigs, geese, hens, ducks, wagons, sleighs, and the proper complement of tools and implements. The cart was made by an elder of the church. Fifty-four years afterwards, as appeared from the Master's books, I sent for this same man to survey the cart, as I suspected it required some repairs. He admitted that the vehicle had not lasted as long as it should, and he feared he "must have put bad stuff in it." He was willing to make the replacements free of charge, as he wished to maintain his reputation for sound work.

Small as it was, this farm was the scene of all human industry. Wool was shorn, carded, spun, and woven into cloth. Cattle were killed. The hides were tanned by one neighbour, made into shoes by another, or into harness by a third. The geese were caught and lightly plucked, so that the feathers might not fall and be wasted. Bread was made from flour, water, and salt — these three elements alone. It was not polluted with fat nor fermented with yeast. It was made light by persistent kneading under the strong hands of a woman.

And these three mills gave to that young world an air of force and activity. In the springtime, when a dam burst and the water flowed away, a boy could walk upon the foundations of the world as if he were Lucifer himself. The upper and the lower mills ground grain of all kinds — wheat, oats, barley, and buckwheat. The middle mill, which was exactly opposite to the gate, sawed timber with upright saws set in gangs. The circular saw had not yet been imported. In that mill from the earliest times was sawn the timber from which many ships were built in shipyards that extended down to deep water. A boy would see the ship launched, and in a year or two news would come that she was cast away on the shores of South America "with the loss of all hands." In earlier days, the founder of the Cunard Line was bottom sawyer to Malcolm Macqueen who gave high praise to his strength and industry. The stumps of the pine trees which these two sawyers cut and sawed are yet to be seen in the woods.

The building of ships demanded many subsidiary industries. Forges clanged the year round. Spars were modelled and canvas was sewn; ropes were made into shrouds, and blocks were shaped. The smell of Stockholm tar spiced the air. This tar in equal parts with port-wine was a sovereign remedy for a cough, and a delectable drink — if the bottle were not shaken, and the wine allowed to come to the top. A cough would last a boy for a whole winter.

Trees were cut and sawn into lumber from which houses were built. Stone was quarried, dressed, and laid up to form cellars. One summer day I found a neighbour in his cellar which was then empty, disclosing its spaciousness and quality; walls thirty feet long, seven feet high, each stone cut to the square and faced with strong even strokes.

"Who quarried the stone ? " I asked.

"I quarried it myself."

"Who cut the stone ? "

"I cut it myself."

"And who laid them up ? "

"I laid them up." He looked upon his work, which was merely an incident in his life; he remembered all his other labours, and said, "No wonder I am in my grave."

The sea was at the door of these early settlers, and yielded of its abundance in the spring when fresh food was needed most. The salmon crowded the rivers; the herring, the gaspereaux, the caplin appeared on the shores in shoals; the trout ascended the streams; the smelt penetrated into the fields and choked the creeks. The smelts were known as *beannachadh*, the blessing. They were the earliest to arrive. Whilst the snow yet lay in sheltered places, they would appear in the streams, a moving shimmering mass against the gravelly bottom, and could be scooped out with a net, more than a boy could carry. They were plentiful beyond the need for food and were used to fertilize the ground. A smelt was planted with each potato seed.

From the sea also came marine grass, kelp, dulse, fit for bedding cattle; fine hay from the marsh, which made fodder and might be used to fill a mattress. A man who looked back upon a long life and surveyed the farm he created would confess that "mussel-mud" was the foundation of his fortune. If the nutritive quality of this fertilizer was less than is supposed, the disciplinary value of dredging it from the sea was precious. In the estuaries were beds of decayed shell fish, ten feet thick. When the ice formed, huge "diggers" were set up, operated by horses. A hole was cut in the ice; a long beam armed at the end with a trip-fork was forced by a rude pawl and rack into the face of the bed. The load was lifted by a capstan, and came to the surface, white shells and black mud dripping with sea water. The treasure was hauled on sleighs far inland and placed in piles upon the snowy fields to be spread in the springtime. For twenty years this shell would dissolve slowly and supply the soil with lime. Assiduity in hauling "mud" was a sign of success, a rite; and it was often put upon land which had no need or could not be improved. One boy, seeing these piles upon an exhausted and abandoned farm, made the judicious observation, "I do not know whether to praise this man for his industry or to reproach him for his folly."

One winter a farmer fell sick of the slow fever. His neighbours assembled to haul mud for him, twenty of them with twenty sleighs and forty horses. The sick man in return was to provide entertainment in the evening for at least forty persons, men and women. As there would be supper of roast ham, boiled beef, baked puddings, infinite pies and cakes, with accessory cream, butter and bread, besides the conventional bottle of liquor for the fiddler, it is not certain that on balance the financial position of the sick man was materially improved, especially as during the day there had been a halt in the proceedings.

When the fork was first lifted a drowned burden was borne to the surface. It was well known that earlier in the year an Indian had "gone through the ice" and perished. Everyone recognized the unfortunate man by the clothes, the long boots, the heavy mitts, the cap drawn over the face and fastened below the chin. The men stood afar off — to windward — whilst a messenger was dispatched for George Sinclair, Justice of the Peace. When the official person arrived, he demanded that the body be laid out upon the ice. It was an effigy that had been attached to the fork during the night by some mischievous boys and lowered into the sea.

A boy learned something of all trades. By continual discipline he received an education of which the "education" in the schools is trifling, absurd, and grotesque; a travesty of the thing itself. This state of inner discipline arose from a systematic obedience to the laws imposed by nature, against which it was useless to contend by force. But the powers of nature could be subdued and directed to human needs by a continuous effort of the mind and will. The boy learned, and was taught, how and within what limits he could bring into service the hardness of metal, the weight of stone, the lightness of wood, the buoyancy of water, the strength of horses, the fertility of domestic animals, and the hidden riches of the soil. By obedience to those inevitable laws he acquired a morality; by developing the feeling of submission and dependence, as one of the forbidden books affirmed, he acquired the rudiments of religion. Then he could profitably go to school and learn from the recorded experience of those who were wiser and older than himself. The school was at hand, and the discipline of the school was not dissevered from the discipline of the home.

This mill was owned by the Master; it was leased to a man called Malcolm Gillis. He played the bagpipes, and wore a Scotch bonnet for the ceremonial. He could not play without that emblem. Twice a year he would come to play his pipes in the dairy to drive away the rats, but he wore the Scotch bonnet. It was long before we learned that music is a thing to be enjoyed for itself and not for any ulterior purpose, such as freedom from rats.

It is well for a man that he bear the yoke in his youth: he gains strength to cast it off. Happy is he who learns fortitude from his parents : he is safe through life. In this old mill one child at least had his first serious lesson in fortitude. The logs were piled on the bank in the winter. With the rising water of the spring each lot of logs was rolled into the pond, and floated by spiked poles to the waste-gate. Each log was guided to the runway that reached down from the mill, wet and slippery, into the water. A dog was driven into the butt-end. To the dog was attached a heavy chain which passed around a spindle controlled by a large wheel armed with iron crotches. A second chain connected this wheel with the main driving wheel of the mill, which lay near the water level twenty feet below. When lateral pressure by a lever was put upon this chain it came to its bearing below and above. The spindle took the chain, and the log came with splash and rush to the saw.

But the vertical chain when not in use would fall free from the lower crotches. It could be brought into place by a series of sidelong swings from above, but the simpler method was for a boy to descend by the timbers of the mill, stand upon the watery wheel, and adjust the chain with his hands. This was reckoned a daring feat, and was eagerly sought. One day a boy saw the chance, and darted down. But the man, unaware of his design, started the mill. The boy felt the wheel turn slowly under his feet. He kept his balance by dancing on the wheel, but the torrent of water threw him off. He must have cried out, although he was afraid of blame for causing the mill to be stopped. In falling he was struck on the head by the iron crotch, was carried insensible down the tail-race by the rushing water, and was finally cast ashore. He felt his father's arms beneath him; they would seem strong and comforting. He carried the child to the house, and said to the mother, "It is a mercy of God." She said not a word. She put the child to bed, and gave him a cake. The blood had been well washed away, and the wound could be left to take care of itself. In a few hours he awoke with an overwhelming sense of the mercy of God. He had allowed the disaster to proceed to such an extremity that the boy was absolved from blame for having stopped the mill.

Life is not life where there is no tragedy. That little world was a world of death — a wild animal caught in a trap, a partridge slain by a hawk, a cow submerged in the marsh, a dog whose time had come; and always the mild-eyed creatures that must be killed for food. Indeed, a boy himself must learn to take part in that ceremonial, and finally to conduct the sacrifice. Thereafter, he was never the same. It was not uncommon to see a boy in tears before the bound animal.

But there was human tragedy too. A neighbour fell sick of typhoid. In his delirium he escaped to the woods, and there died. His body was borne on a truck past the door. The children saw his face and the help-less feet. Even the dog barked in terror. This terror of the dead was the heaviest trial of sensitive boys in the army. "Why are they so cold and stiff?" one boy asked. A party of sappers was detailed to unload wire. The dump was already occupied by rows of the dead. The living enemy inspired less fear. It was un-seemly. The boys were sent away, and the bodies were removed by more experienced hands.

Death is sad; it is not usually malign. Into that

world of Orwell, death came once in the most malignant and malevolent form, and created an atmosphere
of horror. For years after, a woman would not go out
in the dark to take washed clothes from the line. A
man who was compelled to visit his own barn by
night would awaken a child from sleep for the sake
of human company. That same man who entered the
office in Oregon and said, "I only came in to see if
you look like your father — and you do," and having
given his name, his father's name, and the designation
by which he was commonly known, and having specified the farm on which he lived, and left fifty-seven
years ago, made his ultimate talk of that old tragedy.
When he was a boy the scene was familiar to him,
and he had often to pass the spot, riding on the bare
back of a horse. As he came over the rise of ground
even by day he " would shut his eyes, put the whip
to the horse," and never open his eyes until he had
traversed the valley and reached the hill on the opposite side.

The people were coming out of church. They saw
a man running down the slope, bare-footed, and
clad only in shirt and trousers; he was crying in Gaelic, *Na chunnaic mi, na chunnaic mi.* The thing he
saw was the murdered body of his sister. The grandmother, always courageous, was one of the first on
the spot, and she could ever after secure willing service by a promise to tell what it was she saw. What
impressed us most was her description of the heavy
hoe with which the deed had been done, and the
marks of the struggle on the grass.

An enquiry was held in the schoolhouse and the most rigid criminal test applied. All the inhabitants were compelled to lay a hand on the body; but as the body did not bleed afresh, they were all acquitted of the crime, although a certain woman was under suspicion to the end. The body was buried, and there are one or two persons yet living who will point out the grave.

The account given by the Master's wife was more elaborate. Many years afterwards, a man told her that on the night of the crime he was returning from the Bridge. He was a blacksmith by trade, and as he approached his own place, he observed that his forge was ablaze with light and roaring with sound. He thought at first that some traveller had lost a shoe from his horse, and was replacing it by his own skill; but as he came nearer he noticed that two persons were at work, the one shaping the shoe with the small hammer, the other "striking" with the maul. But he observed that the sound of the small hammer was as loud as if it were made by the two-handed maul, and the heavier hammer came down with such strokes as he had never heard. He cried out — and all was still and dark. The moment he saw the fatal hoe, he knew who was the intruder into the forge. The marks of the hammers had been made by no human hand. I have seen the weapon, and the forging did seem heavy. But she was careful to add that a man returning by night from the Bridge would be untrustworthy, and this one was cousin to the woman suspected of the crime.

In the summer of 1930, a woman came to see us. She was daughter to the man upon whose land the body was found, and was the second person who had looked upon the spectacle, her age at the time being thirteen years. She conducted us to the spot, and supplied the minutest details of the tragedy that had occurred seventy-three years ago. It is not probable that anything further will ever be known of the cause or circumstances.

Apart from murder, there was no crime in that community except the crime of going in debt. A man who had stolen cattle was publicly whipped in the market place. A negro sailor who stole bread was hanged at Gallows-point. His crime was wanton : it was proved that he had not eaten the crust. Two boys broke the window of a shop, and extracted three balls of twine. Judge Peters sentenced them to death, on the ground that they had broken into an inhabited house, as the merchant and his family slept above the shop. They were not executed although they were known to be "bad boys." Their sentence was mercifully commuted to twenty-five years imprisonment — and there was no more thieving for a generation. I saw a neighbour carried to gaol with fetters on his feet, as punishment for his failure to pay a debt which had been legally adjudged against him. When imprisonment for debt was abolished, the Master was gravely apprehensive lest worthy men might be denied credit in the hour of their need.

VI

THE MASTER HIMSELF

THE Master, in respect of figure, height, and weight, was the model for a man. He was neither tall nor short, neither heavy nor light. He bore himself erect as a soldier, alert and quick in every movement. He had abundant brown hair, a short and darker beard that whitened early. His head had good bone with a powerful straight nose and small regular white teeth. When he was upwards of seventy one of his sons remarked to him with professional freedom that he had broken the corner of one tooth. "Yes," he admitted, "I did that on a chicken bone. I was wishing to consult you about it. I was afraid it might indicate some weakness in my constitution."

His eyes were clear blue, and his skin of a brilliant whiteness. On his upper arm the letters W. M. were tattooed in purple ink. This gave to him a sense of mystery, and the surmise was that he had fallen into strange company on a desperate voyage he had once made to New York in a schooner. He was a gravely handsome man. His clothes were cut by a good tailor. On the Sabbath he wore broadcloth and a grey beaver hat. The way to church led through a woods, and he would cover the hat with his handkerchief lest a drop of balsam might fall upon it. There is a

THE MASTER

1899

portrait of him by Alphonse Jongers. It hangs in my dining room at the right of my chair, and many a night I have watched his eye looking down upon me from under a slightly drooping lid in mild reproach.

This artist was defined by the Master's wife as "the French gentleman." She would never place herself at the disadvantage of attempting to pronounce a foreign name unless she were quite sure she had achieved complete mastery. Then she would pronounce it slowly with an air of triumph. The Master was a good chess-player. In the evening he played with the artist, but with a sense of wonder that a "foreigner" could play at all. Having won the game, he would conceal his satisfaction, as he put the board away and "took down the books" for family worship, by saying, "I sometimes think this is a sad mis-spending of the few years that are left to me." At the time he was quite well, and lived for ten years more. His wife also played chess, but with a sense of grievance when her opponent captured a piece whose precarious situation she had overlooked.

I had learned the rudiments of the game from Stephen Leacock. We would play in the evening, then before dinner, then before tea. When we began before luncheon and continued all day, we both agreed it was time to abandon the game. My skill was therefore not sufficient to contrive an inevitable stale mate, which she looked upon as the legitimate ending of every game. Checkmate to her was a mark of disrespect, a lack of filial gratitude, proof of an eager, crafty, and grasping mind. To yield checkmate to her she suspected was an act of generosity which she craved but would not admit. She would check her daughters willingly on the ground that she was instructing them in the hazard of the play.

On leaving with the artist and Tait McKenzie the sculptor, the Master's sister, whose name was Janet, met us at the port of departure for a word of greeting. She was easily persuaded to accompany us on the voyage of three hours to the mainland, especially as Captain Cameron with much gallantry asked her to be his official guest. The voyage would not cost her a penny, "nor, indeed, her dinner either." It was at her school he had begun that education which led to his present high estate.

The "French gentleman" was an insatiable reader of English books. His intent was to perfect himself in the language rather than to enrich his mind with their contents, and all books were therefore alike to him. The book at hand the night before was an important and highly controversial work on Infant Baptism by an author whom this aunt respected highly. Here was an opportunity not to be overlooked, to have a European opinion on the subject, an opinion she felt sure, that would be free from any religious prejudice. The artist confessed at once that he thought the book "a complete foolishness." A fresh revelation of the eternal truth of Scripture dawned upon her. She murmured to herself, "To the Greeks the preaching of the Apostle himself was 'foolishness' — and they were artists too."

At the time of purchase the place was burdened

by a mortgage of two hundred pounds, Halifax currency, which was equal to six hundred and fifty dollars. A child old enough to have learned the phrase "skeleton in every closet," asked his mother what our skeleton was. "The big debt," was her prompt answer, although it had then been reduced to three hundred dollars. According to the deed, it was fully paid in the twelfth year. With that little debt discharged, the Master began his financial career and at his death left a fortune of over nine hundred dollars.

And yet, he felt the need of increased security. He established for himself a reserve which he cared for in a trust and loan account. This was a cash reserve, and it was deposited in a wooden safe-deposit box which bore upon the cover the legend written in his own clear and powerful script : *He who giveth to the poor lendeth to the Lord.* He seemed to depend more upon the major security than upon the box, for the box never contained very much, but equally it was never empty. It always contained enough for his contribution to church, missions, religious periodicals, evangelists, and wandering tramps.

At times he was compelled to borrow from this reserve for secular needs, but the amount was scrupulously entered in an account against himself. From the earliest days he recorded all his financial transactions by an elaborate system of book-keeping which involved the use of journal, day-book, and double entry into a ledger. The debits and credits of his dealings with brothers, sisters, and children after they became of mature age are still extant; but his collection department appears to have been weak. There is one last exculpatory entry against his brother who is now in his grave these sixty years : "To close the account, one old hat, two-and-six"; but the account balances perfectly. On rare occasions he appears to have entered upon the perilous career of banker, for there is one despairing entry : "Borrowed from P. MacDonald for .... 10 shillings. If he does not pay it back, I must."

This sum of nine hundred dollars was found intact in the savings account of the Bank of Nova Scotia, an institution which he trusted implicitly. His method of finance was simple, but he never made a loss. He deposited his money at one wicket, where it bore three per cent interest. If he required money to meet some desperate emergency, such as a son's need at the University, he would borrow the amount at the next wicket, and pay six per cent upon the loan. The secret of his system lay in this : the sum borrowed never exceeded the sum on deposit. The late general manager, Thomas Fyshe, often affirmed that a bank, and the country too, would be a happier place if that system were more generally adopted. This wise old banker disclosed from the depth of his experience that he had seen young men lured into crime and old men to ruin by speculation; but he hastened to add that the practice of "buying at the bottom of the market and selling at the top" was not speculation. A judicious combination of the method of the Master and the doctrine of the banker will make any man rich. At any rate, his own system brought to the Master a fulfilment of his daily prayer: that we owe no man anything but to love one another. For twelve years he had become so habituated to this form of words that he could not omit them wholly, even after the debt was paid and his savings accumulated in the bank. He did however change the form from supplication to giving of thanks.

When he became Inspector of Schools, he enjoyed a salary of six hundred dollars a year. After fifteen years the modern system of education began to emerge. Every school, scholar, and teacher must be rigidly graded; and even a teacher must attend a school with the design that he be taught how to teach. If Plato or Socrates were upon the earth, they would not be allowed to teach unless they could produce a certificate in "pedagogy"; and if Shakespeare were teaching English he would be dismissed from his post on the ground that he had not passed an examination. The Master refused to submit, although it was suggested to him that the process would be only *pro forma*.

About the same time a scandal occurred in the public hospital for insane. Two attendants had gravely mishandled a patient who was of a contrary faith; and an official had diverted supplies to his own use. The government was shaken by the clamour, and they saved themselves by appointing the Inspector as Supervisor at the increased salary of seven hundred dollars. He performed those duties under successive governments until near the end of his life with a rigid integrity. He was master once more.

The Premier came one Sabbath morning to make a formal official inspection. The Supervisor refused to accompany him. He handed over his keys and records. He recommended the Premier to make his own inspection, and record his observations in the usual book under the exact date. The Premier was a wise man. He postponed his inspection. He had no desire to engage in a controversy with Highlanders upon the delicate ground of Sabbath observance. It is a matter for surmise to what extent, if any, the Master was fortified by the knowledge that the Premier was Irish and Catholic.

Everything the Master did was correct — his manner of eating, of drinking, of holding a pen or a book, of sitting on a chair or arising from it; and he did his best to instil a sense of correctness in his children. A child who was too tired or too indolent to sit erect was allowed the option of going to bed. To "sprawl in a chair" was to him the mark of a slovenly and undisciplined mind. He had words of deadly directness. To stroll on a forest path with motive ulterior to the purpose of passing through was "to lurk in the woods." For a boy to proceed at any other pace than a run was to linger, loiter, dawdle, meander, creep, saunter. He had the gift of vivid narrative. The slightest incident gained interest and charm by the dramatic quality he bestowed upon it. On a journey to the town he would find material for an evening's entertainment. By contrast, the mother professed to believe that we might as well be blind and dumb, for all we could see and tell.

The Master took no part in public affairs. He was so anxious to render unto God the things that were God's that he felt his full duty towards Caesar performed when he paid his taxes and cast his vote for any Tory candidate who might present himself for election. On such occasions he would drive to the polling place which was a high covered platform open to the world. An official would demand in a loud voice the name of the candidate for whom he desired to vote, and the Master would speak the Tory name in a tone of pride for all the world to hear. Fumbling with a pencil and ballot in a dark and secret corner he thought a base and cowardly practice more suitable for conspirators than for free men. On one occasion he was chosen to preside at a joint political meeting. An incautious elector asked his opinion of the issue. He replied that he was there to keep order, not to offer opinions or give advice. He always praised himself for that judicious answer.

The Master was a mild man, ever careful to abstain from harsh or final judgements. When his opinion was sought upon a candidate for the ministry, the utmost of his affirmation was : We must not set bounds to the mercy of God; but if this student should become a spiritually minded man, that would be proof of His providence and power. With more mature minds, we began to suspect that these elaborate replies and sonorous sentences were framed for his own intellectual pleasure in the precise use of words, to administer a rebuke in mildest form, or even to point a jest. An American tourist passing a funeral enquired the name of the victim. On the ground that any one having a rational interest in the matter would already have known the name, and otherwise would be none the wiser even if he were told, he received as a rebuke for his curiosity : Every man is dead, who is yet in his trespass and his sin. Humour, like a living stream, will find a way to the light.

There was a suspicion too, that the Master encouraged this dialectic as a barrier against trivial, futile, and foolish talk, in precisely the same way that one will now turn on the radio machine when his visitors threaten to become tiresome. And it was an exercise in which all the men could engage, the women observing the silence of custom, and children of obligation. A man without the necessary learning and experience to bear the main theme could support it by a judicious comment or text; he could signify his comprehension of the Augustinian doctrine of grace by the single fervent phrase, "not of our own merits," and his dissent from the doctrine of works and sacerdotalism, "in the twinkling of an eye," to indicate the ease and speed of final forgiveness. Sir Robert Walpole also discovered the value of the specific subject; at his table he encouraged a peculiarly primitive kind of talk, a conversation in which every gentleman could join. For one who kept silence there was always the excuse that a man could not go ahead of his light.

The handling of these high themes made his children familiar with good words, rich phrases, and the powerful thought contained in elaborate texts. They were initiated into the intellectual and literary life to which their scholastic studies were soon discovered as a means to further entrance. Indeed an understanding of the doctrine of the Trinity gave a sense of reality to the deeper parts of the arithmetic, to the axioms of geometry, and to algebraical symbols.

But there were not wanting those who practised the theological art for their private humour and their personal gain. In preparation for one of those additions to the old house, a distant man was found to cut timber in the woods. He was willing to come at a monthly wage and subsistence, but he admitted frankly that he was at the moment under conviction of sin, and could not give full attention to any earthly task. The Master too was willing. Credit would come to him if the catechumen were set free in his house. In those discussions this man was the most forward with comment and texts; but even a child could observe that his texts, instead of supporting the main position, were contrary and destructive. In the morning he lay long abed, but his voice in prayer pervaded the house. As he affected inability to read, he would persuade a child to accompany him to the woods to search and read the Scriptures for him until finally, overcome by emotion, he would fall asleep in a shady nook. The Master was well aware of the tossing to and fro of the sinner in the watches of the night, but he was more concerned with the slowness of the conversion than with the small pile of timber. When his wife informed him from her own observation and on the authority of one of her own people, that the man was a mocker, and a drunkard in secret, the Master was not disturbed. He had at last seen one who had been handed over to the power of Satan to be destroyed. But the enlargement of the house was delayed until the following year.

VII

THE WORLD OF SIN

THE Master had so little sin in his own life and world that he was compelled to create imaginary sins, so that the miracle of his redemption should be the more complete. That is the way of all good men. For the same reason the Apostle declared himself to be the chief of sinners. In this forgiveness of sin that had no existence there was menace to the young. The forgiveness of actual sin was too easy; it became automatic. In the act itself, it was believed, a kind of antitoxin was developed, which destroyed the original virus as in a physical disease.

From forgiveness, by the mere asking, of a sin already committed, it was an easy deduction to seek forgiveness in advance of a sin one proposed to commit. This was the Antinomian heresy of John Agricola, and it flourished in that community. It came to be believed that as the elect cannot fall from grace, or forfeit the divine favour, the wicked actions they commit are not really sinful, and that consequently they have no need to confess their sins and make repentance. There was yet a more dangerous inference, that such a one was free to continue in the performance of sinful acts and even to engage in others to which one might be inclined. A famous elder in the church, who had an infirmity for drink, was reputed to arise all the brighter from his periodical indulgences.

A child, although he never went the length of taking an apple from the tree, would in that fancied security shake the tree and bring apples to the ground, trusting to receive a share of the spoil from the one who found them, and so profit from the crime. There were three apple trees in the garden when the Master acquired the place. They must now be a hundred years old, and one still bears fruit of a delicate sweetness. They were a continual temptation to the young of the neighbours, which was only too imperfectly resisted. Indeed those marauders were known to share their spoil with us who might be supposed to have a better right. This sophistry led in due course to actual transgression, but with facile assurance in that remedy which could be applied to it as well as to original sin.

To a child this doctrine of duality is incomprehensible. He cannot distinguish between conduct and a state of mind, between the Jacobean covenant of works and the Augustinian state of grace. In this confusion, he may come to believe that he can pursue a downward course of conduct by nicely graded steps and draw back when danger threatens. He never suspects that he may suddenly lose his foothold and plunge into the abyss. Parents who intrude these theoretical conceptions, commonly called evangelical, into the innocence of childhood assume a heavy responsibility for the passive defiance or secret hypocrisy that may result.

The Master believed firmly in the efficacy of prayer. It would remove mountains and equally the pain of a child's accident. He would lay his hand upon the injured part, and the youngest child could observe from the closed eyes and murmuring words that he was the victim of an incantation. In fear of the unknown, in shame at being the witness of an emotion, in the desire to assist at a miracle, the child would cease his crying and declare that he was instantly healed. In any event the prayer was answered; but the child suffered a deeper hurt.

The mind of a child is the mind of a dreamer by night. Things remembered, and unrelated, are joined in a fantastic sequence. He begins with a set of illusions from which fresh and logical illusions are developed, but the whole figment has the force of intense reality. Some fifteen miles away was a marvellous garden of apples. Every year the Master's wife made a visit to the place, for the eldest son of the owner was married to her sister. Each child was taken in turn, and it was the principal event in his young life. When the scene burst upon me, I knew this was the original garden. It lay to the eastward; in it grew every tree that was pleasant to the sight; and a noble river went out from it. Towering over all was a painted sign of warning, that a spring gun and man-trap was set there; and yet I entered in and did eat.

The owner bore the ominous name, Roger Dart Westaway. I was brought before him in the cool of

the day. He was an ancient bearded man; he sat upon an elaborate chair, resting his hands upon a powerful stick. He took me between his knees, and regarded me in awful silence. Then he made a jocular remark which betrayed his knowledge. So, this was the
man-trap. He was discerning the thoughts and in-
tents of the heart, and the actual transgression in
respect of his apples; his stick was the "dart" of his
name, by which he could divide asunder the soul
and the spirit, the joints and the marrow. I knew
him for Whom he was, and ever after I understood
how fearful a thing it is to fall into the hands of the
living God. The experience, however, did not deter
me, when I was released, from continuing to eat his
apples until my teeth were set on edge, and I met the
final bar of pain. There was a limit then, it appeared,
to human happiness, and a consequent punishment
for excess.

The Master's wife, without actually invoking the
practice and tradition of her own family, created a
healthy scepticism of these other-worldly devices and
conceptions. The occasional visits of her old uncles
cleared the air. A visit to them gave entrance into a
wholesome and real world. They would even instruct
a boy in the posture he was to assume and the language he was to employ if he were molested by a
bigger boy on the road. The mother never wavered
in the belief that her own people required no special
act of grace; they were immune from evil in virtue
of their own nature and practice; their strength was
increased by using the good things of this world;

self-denial was for the weak and timorous. They even boasted that they were not afraid of the devil; he did not interest them. It was a secret pleasure to her that her own sons were disposed to follow the way of her own people.

To an aged cousin of hers I sent a case of whisky which, he admitted to her with tears in his eyes, was the only present he had ever received in his life. Within two weeks, when she passed that way, he lamented he had no drink to offer her. "Friends had come in" — that was explanation enough. In two weeks more he too was dead.

I asked her if she thought there was any connexion between the gift and the sad event. She had a way of expressing indignation. She would sit up very straight, nod her head, and flash her mild brown eyes. I had gone too far. "None of my people were ever affected by liquor," she protested. She always adhered to the opinion that liquor "did a person nothing but good; it brought out the best that was in them." Indeed, she had never known it to do harm to any one, unless possibly to a man she had heard of when she was a girl, who, coming home late from a party, sat down on his wood-pile to rest, and was found dead in the morning. "But," she offered as explanation of the strange occurrence, "it was winter time, and he might have perished from the cold."

On the other hand, she had observed that the sudden abandonment of the practice — and such cases were known — was certainly the sign and probably the cause of approaching death. She was

bitter against women who kept liquor away from
their men. It was foolish and cruel. A man himself
knew best when he had enough; but she would allow
the woman to secrete a little for him against the
morning. A relation of her own, who had grown old
and blind, was so restricted by "the young woman,"
that he was compelled to measure with his finger in
the glass, lest he might be defrauded; and she was
especially bitter against that one.

It is probably true that certain families have an
immunity against alcohol. A cousin of her own came
to dinner. He was upwards of eighty years old at the
time, with a noble forehead, a nose all bone, and a
beard broad as a spade. He sat on my left and I
passed the decanter to him. He poured gently but
firmly until the tumbler was exactly two-thirds full.
I feared he was absent-minded, but she warned me
with her eye. I was at a loss to know how he would
proceed. He spurned the water; indeed there was
hardly room in the glass for it; he could not swallow
the drink at a single draught, as the custom of some
was; nor could he follow the practice ascribed to us,
which was to add plenty water and drink as if it were
tea. He drank as a hungry child would drink milk,
slowly, gently to the bottom. I looked that he would
fall down dead, but nothing happened, except an
excess of geniality which she regarded as a triumph
for her doctrine.

It was a source of continuous pride to her that
this immunity against alcohol had been transmitted
unimpaired to her sons; that gift is yet a source of

wonder to their children. It is her youngest son who is so gifted in the highest degree. When he was quite young he had come off a hard cold journey, and was restoring himself with an equal mixture of brandy and port-wine. His mother was apprehensive lest he should take harm from the wine.

" 'Strong drink' " he assured her, " 'for him who is ready to perish, and wine for him who is heavy of heart.' I am in both conditions; I am drinking brandy and wine in equal proportions."

His father, who by this time was somewhat broken in spirit by the imponderable forces of this world, interposed a mild objection against the brandy.

"Do not be too hard on him" she pleaded, "he is the youngest" — for to be the last of a large family was excuse for any eccentricity. Then by a great effort of thought the boy repeated :

"I am of those to whom the promise is given, 'He shall take up any deadly thing, and it shall not come nigh unto him.' " He long lamented that he had failed to push his advantage by reciting the dogma, "It is not that which enters into a man defileth him, but the words that proceed out of his mouth."

The Master himself had long since abandoned his modest drink. When the wave of prohibition began to flow, he was one of the first to succumb, and he was fond of relating the reason for his decision. He had met a friend, one of the Comptons, at the Bridge. They had half a glass of pale brandy; and in accordance with the deplorable practice of treating they had one more. No ill effects were apparent at

the time, so subtle is the demon. But some days afterwards, he had a dream of which he remembered
certain fantastic elements. He confessed with some
pride that this mental disturbance might be the initial
sign of that final condition commonly called "the
horrors." His wife warned him that people might
believe him, and in future he kept his experience to
himself.

She thought that alcohol aroused the sense of sin,
which in turn brought repentance. She believed, further, that sin ran through humanity like a well ordered little stream; if it were suddenly damned back in
any one generation, it would be sure to break bounds,
and devastate the succeeding one.

No atheist was ever known to have come within
that house, although isolated specimens of the breed
were said to exist in the town not more than twenty
miles away. An alert Elder spent a Sunday afternoon
describing an encounter he had, and the dialectical
triumph he achieved. If the personage had been a
witch or a devil, the narrative could not have been
more interesting. He began the performance by a
statement of his own position which he had presented
in opening the contest. All mankind, being descended from Adam, sinned in him and fell with him,
whereby they lost communion with God, and so were
made liable to all miseries in this life, to death itself,
and to the pains of hell forever; but God, out of his
mere good pleasure, having elected some to everlasting life, entered into a convenant of grace to
deliver them and to bring them into an estate of sal-

vation by a Redeemer. All this was very tiresome, as it was so well known. The Master showed some impatience, and his wife went about her household duties.

But interest revived when the Elder began to define the position of the atheist. He was willing to accept the dogma in respect of original sin. In respect of any sin which he himself might commit, he was determined to stand upon his own feet. He denied utterly that he sinned daily in thought word and deed. Every night, he called himself to account before God for his conduct during the day; and he never fell asleep without assurance that the account was squared. The Elder then put the atheist in mind of hell. His reply was that no threat of torment, or even torment itself, would extort from him a confession of guilt which he did not feel; and he called to his support the experience of the martyrs.

"He could not then be an atheist," the Master interposed, "if he called himself to account before God."

"He may be only a Free-thinker; but it is Atheist they call him," the Elder explained.

The Master's wife, who never took part in these discussions, returned in time to hear the atheist's final defiance, that he did not believe in hell. She interposed the charitable remark, that disbelief in hell was not the same as disbelief in God. This brought from the Elder a further disclosure of the atheist's mind. He professed a belief in a place intermediate between hell and heaven. He was not bad enough for hell, nor good enough for heaven. This was "his own place" for which he hoped, until he should be purified, as one might be willing to go to the gaol for his own good, but not to the gallows. One would suppose to hear him talk, the Elder continued, that God was not more harsh than Judge Peters.

"I do not think he is," she observed mildly.

"That is the doctrine of the Smiths," the Elder broke out, and came upon dangerous ground even in the Master's house.

"The Smiths are as likely to be right as the — —." She named the family name of the Elder. "Come children," she concluded, "Your supper is ready." We followed her with a strange comfort in the courage of the atheist and in the leniency of her judgement. "Come children," clearly meant that the Master and the Elder were free to continue the discussion if they wished. It was equally clear that they might go hungry, if they did. She also managed to convey the suggestion that hell need not be taken so seriously, when the subject could be dismissed by calling her children to supper.

VIII

HIS MOTHER

MARY Macpherson was the grandmother. I saw her for the first time not in the Master's house but in the house of her younger son, who was called James. He was teaching school at the Whim Road, ten miles off, and she lived with him. This James had broken away from the traditional occupation, and went to sea. In the West Indies he went ashore on the island of Nassau, and climbed a palm-tree for coconuts, fell, and broke his arm. It was on the Sabbath day. At the end of the voyage he was admitted into the Seaman's Hospital in Brooklyn; but the fracture was compound, and never healed. He came home, resumed his proper occupation, and soon died.

When I saw him, a pale invalid, sitting in his chair, with his long dark beard, I looked upon him as if he were Tantalus under the divine wrath; for it was on the Sabbath day he had climbed the tree. It was the winter time, and coming home at night I fell asleep on the bottom of the sleigh under the buffalo robe, and descending a steep bank rolled forward, as I thought, into some bottomless pit with this uncle for sole companion.

Sixty years passed. In a letter received from that young wrestler, dated February 3, 1926, and posted in Havana, he makes mention of this incident of which he had been informed. He also arrived at Nassau on the Sabbath; he desired a coconut, but he was careful to engage a black boy to climb the tree. In that same letter, too, he disclosed that he had the power to penetrate to the heart of an adventure. Upon that new voyage into a tropical world he could neglect the extraneous and discern a man : "There is little English spoken aboard this ship; only American and Scotch. The ship sailed from Glasgow and embarked her passengers in New York. The purser is a black Munro from Argyll. He spoke to me one evening. There was casual talk for a few minutes until he enquired, 'Have you the Gaelic ? ' I replied with my only phrase, to which he made some response in that tongue. Within five minutes I was in his cabin taking a drink. He disclosed to me the inner places of his heart, wherein I found that his chief desire was, before he died, to write a piece of prose, to make a sonnet, to paint a picture, and to compose a piece of music. The first is done: he had two pieces of prose published in *Chamber's Magazine*; his sonnet was accepted by the *Atlantic Monthly,* but when he received the proof he began to perfect it, and it has never appeared. The third ambition is represented by some watercolours in his cabin — but only as a beginning — and the fourth is not yet accomplished or begun."

The grandmother was glad to see her son and his child. Her ruddy face glowed with pleasure, and she laughed aloud. I was not aware an old woman could laugh. The Master's wife never laughed; and if she smiled it was not from simple pleasure; there was in the smile an intellectual reminiscent quality, a comment, critical, ironical, or sardonic. When she lay dead, all remarked that there was upon her face an expression of mild and gentle disapproval of the helpless situation in which she found herself.

Mary Macpherson never excelled in housework. She expected to have things done for her, and if they were not done, her quiet content remained undisturbed. In her father's house there had been servants. She sometimes spoke of a cook, who was dismissed from her place because she "would not cool the porridge with the meal"; and of dairy maids who would take her as a child for a week into the hills where they tended the cattle, of which "there were seventy-six to be milked," and from the milk, cheese and butter made.

The Master's wife was sceptical of such "stories." She had never heard of "shielings," or the upland pastures to which Highland cattle were driven for the summer grass. Still less did she believe that there was ever such a person as "Lady Cluny," who would invite young girls to "a party, where there would be dancing, for three days at a time." But when a serious and truthful man arrived from Scotland, and attested from his own knowledge that all these things were so, she was compelled — and secretly proud — to believe.

It was the custom of the country for a woman, as soon as she became a mother-in-law, "to take to the chair," to sit in silence, contenting herself with the wheel, the care of a child, and a bit of knitting, leaving the administration of the house to "the young woman." This grandmother never took to the chair, and in that resolve her three daughters on their spasmodic return from their schools openly abetted her. To this subversion of custom the Master's wife exerted a most passive resistance. She never raised her voice, but she never yielded, not even to the combined force of those four women. So passive was her resistance, the Master remained an innocent neutral, unaware of the conflict in his own house.

On one occasion from a sense of duty he remonstrated with his wife for "working until three o'clock on the Sabbath morning." The Minister was staying in the house, and his white shirts must be prepared by no other hand than hers, as if she were assisting at some hierophantic rite. These shirts had ruffled fronts, and required the delicate use of starch and an elaborate "smoothing-iron." The starch was prepared by scraping the whitest of potatoes, and allowing the grains of starch to settle down several times in cold water which must be frequently renewed. The process occupied three hours, and all was arranged to have the shirts finished by twelve o'clock. But an accident happened to the starch, and to make a new supply demanded three of the forbidden hours. She bore the remonstrance with an appearance of meekness. She did not even tell him it was his own mother who had innocently thrown out the starch, as she required the bowl for a drink before she went to bed.

THE GRANDMOTHER

On public occasions the grandmother wore silk, with a white frill under a satin hood secured by long streamers of the same. There is a portrait of her in that costume, drawn by Dyonnet — but from a photograph only. She was "a bold woman." She would speak to any man, and the proper persons she would address by their first names. The whole fabric of my social edifice came down when I once heard her call the merchant "Denis," although that was his baptismal name, and threaten "to throw his goods about his feet." Her authority in the settlement was greater than in the house. She was said to be an accomplice of all who did not take life as the somber preparation for a life to come which was reputed to be only a little less somber than this. The Irish were her especial friends.

One day she was returning from the town in the little steamer, properly arrayed, and sitting alone in the "ladies" cabin. Two men came in with a bottle from which they proposed to drink. They had already been drinking, and were unperturbed by the spectacle of the silken woman.

"What did you say to them ? "

"I said, 'I will take a drop of that myself.' " That formula is used in the family until this day.

Mary Macpherson's one superior authority was witches. The Smiths, it is true, were also at times, but not grievously, afflicted by witchcraft. The evil usually fell upon their horses, although they were notoriously idle and well fed. One of the old men would take a flail and thresh out their daily ration of oats, which was considered better for them than the product of the machine. Our own family by the precaution of the mother was fairly free from the effects of witchcraft. When she saw a woman of well-known repute coming to the house, she would remove the churn to the cellar, or a young child to some secret place, although all of us had surreptitiously received from Irish neighbours the protection conferred upon their own children. She always knew why one of them was taken for a moment into "the spare room." She could taste the salt on their heads; but she allowed that "the holy water," if it did them no good, would do them no harm.

It was easier to avoid a spell than to remove it once it had been cast, although she was quite familiar with the best practice of exorcism. A piece of silver was put into a white bowl, and the bowl allowed to fill from a running spring. The vessel was turned slowly, and "suitable words" were spoken, until the contents were poured over the afflicted animal. A threepenny bit of silver was used; it was the smallest silver coin, and the exorciser always retained it as a fee for the service.

It was a common event of a morning to see a horse in a sweat, with tangled mane where a witch might well have clung during her nightly ride. Ghosts were too common to excite much interest; and the fairies all seemed so malignant that the grandmother found it difficult to explain the distinction between a fairy and a witch. The Master himself was once smitten in the leg by a fairy-dart, as he was mounting a horse. Tennis players are yet at times so afflicted, but they ascribe the accident to a rupture of the *plantaris* muscle.

It was in stories of forays, robberies, and murders that this Highland woman excelled; but she had many songs and ballads in which the more important events were recorded; and they were mainly derogatory of all clans but her own. Some of these "murder stories" I found printed in a book one wet afternoon in Inverness, exactly as she told them. In one case, as an appendix occupying fourteen pages, was the sermon preached before the execution. These diversions of hers were not encouraged; they were a waste of time and a seduction from important tasks.

These stories must have been authentic. They are to be found in the old books, as one continually discovers. Of these the most specific was the account of the Witch-woman of the Cairngorm Hills. She had taken the form of a gigantic cat and attempted the life of a hunter. By some contrary magic he gave her a mortal wound. She fled home to her cottage and, resuming her natural form, died in the presence of her neighbours. At the hour of her death, a shepherd was walking from Dalarossie, where there is a church-yard so holy that all magic and witchcraft lose their power. A woman passed him running for refuge. She was desperately wounded in throat and breast. Following her was a black man on a black horse, riding hard with two black hounds in full cry. Before long the shepherd was overtaken by the same crew; but now the black man carried the body of the woman across his saddle-bow with the dogs clinging by their teeth. The soul of the witch had sought sanctuary in the sacred enclosure, but was overtaken and carried off to its own place. For children these were rich stories.

The grandmother was the one authority upon all matters that lay beyond our little Island world. She was of "the old country"; she had crossed the sea, and all knowledge was imputed to her. What did a mountain look like? Did it rise up from the level ground? Or, was it approached by lesser mountains? How high were the waves of the sea? And how could they wreck a ship? The answers to these questions occupied many a winter evening, and created a profound unrest in young minds.

She had some gift in the simpler forms of music, and could sing in a shrill and true voice. The song she sang best was the poignant "I'm wearin' awa' John." The confident assertion, "And angels beckon me to the land o' the leal," the Master heard without entire approval. He was not convinced of the "grounds of her assurance," in view of the meagreness of "the profession" the dying woman had made.

Many of those "professions" continue to have a somewhat flimsy basis. Alexander Blair, not so many years ago, went to New York in company with a railroad official who was entitled to travel in a private car. At dinner in a restaurant, he fell dead on the floor. It appears that in New York there are places called "cabarets," where one may eat a section of the meal, and dance in the intervals of service. That was the scene of his death. In conversation with the minister who conducted the funeral, I suggested that, if a man were free to choose the hour and article of his death, he would prefer some other place; and I asked if Sandy Blair had made any "profession of religion." The minister assured me that he had, and furnished the proof :

"He borrowed from me not a month before he died Strachan's *Sermons on the Book of Job.*" There was no evidence that he had read the book; certainly he had not returned it.

The Master's wife resented the elder woman's talk of foreign parts. She surmised that it contained an implied criticism of her insularity. She had "no desire to travel." The limit of her ambition was to sail around the Island, and in time such a voyage was contrived for her; but when the circuit was half made, she suffered from the nemesis of fulfilled desire and demanded that she be put ashore.

This proclaimed fixture of tenure was a rebuke to the wandering habits of that family with which she had become involved. Her own husband had sailed to New York in a schooner. The diary of his doings is yet extant. One of his sisters had ventured as far as Port Daniel in a vessel going for lumber. All three of them later in life to no good purpose went to Missouri and then to Texas with the intention of living there; but they all returned to die.

This diary is barren of comment upon that great city, except for an item which explains the silence. The third day he went ashore, he was accosted by a

young woman with an air of familiarity and friendship. As he was a complete stranger in those parts,
he enquired of the woman if she too had "come from
the Island." It appears that there was in the vicinity
another "Island" of less high repute. The woman for
no reason apparent to him took sudden offence, and
applied to him "most injurious language in a loud
and coarse voice. She was a desperate character."
He sought refuge on his ship which he never left
whilst he remained in that port.

The Master's wife had it from Captain Cameron
that travelled persons used their experience to demonstrate their superiority. His own first adventure
was with a load of lumber to the River, that is, to
the River Rio de La Plata in Buenos Aires, commonly
called "The Plate." He was less than twenty years
of age when he went thither, as master of a ship,
sailing out of Tatamagouche in Nova Scotia, with a
crew composed of other boys who were his own
relations or friends. As he told the story, he would
recite their names and specify their exact relationship to himself but that is not material to the present
illustration.

They were wind-bound at the River, and one
night were "sitting in," that is, drinking rum. There
were at least thirty captains present, all deep sea
sailors; and their talk was of rounding the Horn, of
the Black Current and the White Current; of ice-
bergs, shoals, and reefs. It was quite clear the conversation was directed against these "Island boys," in
contempt of their inexperience. When the situation

became intolerable, his cousin "Big Isaac," addressed him as "Captain," although he usually called him "Sandy" : "Does it not blow like hell off Cape Bear?" This, it appears, is one of the main promontories of Prince Edward Island, and the home of some of those boys. Captain Cameron thought it "a very good answer, and after that there was not a word." Amongst Highlanders there is always a suspicion of offence.

On the return voyage Captain Cameron lost his reckoning, and ran down to a steamer which he sighted. He hailed the stranger.

"Where are you from ? "

"From Hong Kong — in China," as if "I did not know where Hong Kong was."

"Where are you from ? "

"From Tatamagouche — and try if you will find out where that is." With this retort, Captain Cameron squared away, "and to hell with the reckoning."

Although this talk of foreign parts was an extreme irritation to the Master's wife as a veiled criticism of her stability, late in life she herself became something of a traveller; but she would confess to the aberration with a sense of shame. The only explanation she could offer was that she must have been bewitched. She was prevailed upon to accompany the Master on a voyage to Boston. By night the sea arose. She was afraid, and sought the larger refuge of the cabin, where she sat alone in the darkness, reflecting upon her folly. In Boston the streets were hard and painful; "trains and trams were a mean way of

travelling"; they governed one's movements; one had
no liberty to go or to come as one desired. Finally,
she observed in the suburbs of Boston a spectacle
that brought her to her senses. This was a horse and
wagon, tied to a white fence in front of a garden.
How happy that man must be. Then she remembered that she herself had all those possessions at Orwell
— horses, wagons, white fence, and garden. She left
for home next day.

One year, she came to Montreal with the design
of living with me for the winter. I had a large and
extremely handsome house-maid who in her volum-
inous white aprons "looked like a ship under full
sail." She questioned me closely as to how many
maids I kept, the nature and extent of their duties,
and the wages they received. She soon discovered
that, in addition, a "Frenchman" came daily to do the
work that might well be left to the women, and worst
of all, they did not even wash their own clothes. As
if it were a question of mere abstract economic interest, she enquired into the number of white aprons
they wore in a week and the cost of washing them
at the public laundry. I strove to exculpate myself
by dividing the number by three and the cost by four;
but even at that she was making a mental calculation.
I protested my helplessness; but she soon went home,
and there announced that she could not live in a
house where there was so much scandalous waste,
and she powerless to prevent it.

And yet, the following year, I encountered her in
New York. living in rather an elaborate hotel with

her daughter who was visiting a rich but eccentric woman who would spend a holiday in no other place than Orwell. At luncheon, her napkin "large enough for a table cloth" fell from her silk dress to the floor. The waiter "whipped it up," and provided a fresh one. "If the man had to wash it himself, he would not be so smart," she said. In the afternoon we went to a place called the Hippodrome, then newly opened. There was a splendid display, described as "the garden of flowers" — young women constructed to look like pansies, roses, lilies; and others like butterflies and birds that hovered and flew from unobserved steel wires. She was pleased beyond measure; but of a sudden she made a frightful discovery. "They are alive; they are living. Let us get out of this," she whispered in shame and alarm to her daughter. They went — and I went too.

The Master had a larger ambition of travel. It was his one wordly desire to visit the Holy Land, but he was not permitted to enter in. He had neither time nor means. Many years later his desire was fulfilled vicariously. Four of his sons made the pilgrimage together. He would have regarded as a miracle, that there should be four brothers, that they should desire to go, that they should wish to travel in company, that they should remain in unity for so long a time; and finally that they should have had leisure and money for so vast an undertaking.

The almoner at the Hospice at Jerusalem where we lodged was perplexed by the conjunction of consonants in our name, and imagined we were Poles.

Pourquoi non 'f' ? he asked. Avoiding the difficulty, he rendered the bill — and it was not a small one — to *Les quatre frères*. We conceived the idea of re-founding the church, and adopted the most ancient earthly authority, beyond the Mohamedan, Christian, or Jewish religion. The legend then ran : *L'église des quatre frères d'après l'ordre de Melchisedeck.*

The first addition to the number was Lord Beaverbrook who made his own pilgrimage the following year. Herein is recorded for the first time the reason for his irreproachable conduct since that event.

A younger member of the party was chagrined that our host in London should be so ill defended against the cold, and sent to him from Winnipeg a handsome pair of buffalo robes. Each robe had a small chain and padlock by which it could be secured to a stanchion in the motor car. The giver was careful to explain that this means of security was a comment upon the habits of the West and not upon the friends of the noble lord.

IX

THE OLD HOUSE

THE house at Orwell was correct in design and of sound construction. The main part is yet intact after a hundred years, although it has submitted to many replacements, repairs, and additions. There was a front door with two windows on each side. From the hall four rooms opened, and a stair ascended. This hall extended into the kitchen which, with pantries, and store room above, formed an extension to the main structure. All houses were of that design : the size was governed by the means of the builder. They required no architect's plan. In later years it was thought remarkable "that a picture should be made in advance of the building."

A little to the west was the site of an older house, marked by a hollow, and an apple-tree that bore fruit so sour that it protected itself against the hardiest boy. All houses were set to "Captain Holland's compass," which was far to the west of what is now magnetic north. To this day all new houses are set to the same mark, so that the front may be parallel with the road.

These wooden houses, if protected from the weather, attain to a great age. They can easily be hauled to a new site, and are an article of commerce like a vehicle or a horse. A small house built of hewn timber 115 years ago found its final resting place in our garden. It was first occupied by a tailor, his family below, his shop above, reached by a ladder without. A child of the younger generation adopted it as his own. With the help of his sister he shingled the roof; with the help of a carpenter he laid the birch floor, and secured himself with a hasp, staple and padlock. When news arrived that a cousin had been born, he was observed diligently working with a screw-driver to raise the fastening of the door by a foot. He was protected for some years at least against the young intruder. The Master's wife commended him. "One must be master in his own house," she said.

Remote as was that old house, it was in a world of correct behaviour. The truth is, the Highlanders were the last community of gentlemen. Ignorant people express surprise that the Young Prince went unscathed for nine months with the price of thirty thousand pounds upon his head. He lived among his own, and gentlemen do not betray their own. It was by the Lowlanders his more famous ancester had been betrayed to his death. Besides, these people at Orwell lived upon their own land in their own houses, and correct behaviour is inseparable from that high estate.

Those who enter a house in which an old man, a Highlander, master of the house, was born, would do well to attend to their manners. Against that background any flaw is too apparent. The one who most triumphantly endured the test was Lord Grey. He was once at Orwell, and in the party were Lord Percy, later the Duke of Northumberland, Lord Lanesborough, L. S. Amery, John McCrae, Lady Grey, Lady Evelyn, and others. He wandered across the fields in company with some of his friends, and entered upon the land of a neighbour, John Macqueen, who at the moment was busy in his barn with a fork in his hand.

As we entered the barn, I presented him to Lord Grey, as to the Governor-General; and he in turn introduced his friends to his host. After the few correct words of devotion, fidelity, and allegiance to the person of his Sovereign, and a generous welcome to all, this man with his fork strewed clean yellow straw on the high sill of the barn, whereon we sat, and continued the conversation. At the proper moment he invited Lord Grey within his house, but him alone. He left us where we were without a word of apology. He gave us the credit of sharing in his own subtle perception that we would consider ourselves something less than worthy of taking immediate part in the august ceremonial of the entrance of His Majesty beneath his roof. But he soon came back and bade us in turn to enter.

Lord Grey ever after referred to John Macqueen as "the old gentleman," and to his wife as " a picture by Holbein." "That is a fine man, Lord Grey; he has the heart of a farmer," was the opinion from the other side; and he added with the precision of the Gaelic subjunctive and literalness of words, "If sixty years ago I had been told that the Governor-General at any future time should come under my roof, I

would have said that my informant was either a liar
or a fool."

The house at Orwell was not without the means
of culture. There was a sense of good order and mild
dignity. The Master was correctly considered a
Christian gentleman — those were the words by
which public opinion agreed to describe him; the
Master's wife lived up to the esteem in which she
was held. There is no culture when people are engrossed in material things; it thrives only in the higher regions, with literature, music, and religion. Of
religion there was no lack; there was something also
of the other arts. Wherever the Master found himself, by instinct, and unconsciously, he set up a school
of manners. He brought with him an air of refinement and a savour of good.

The house was not without books. A public library had been established by the Fletchers. It could
not have had many subscribers, and when they left
the place the books were distributed by lot. Some
fell to the Master, but there was nothing more recent
than Macaulay's *History of England*, Moore's *Poems*,
and *Edwards on The Trinity*. Our own Minister was
an author of some repute, and his three works were
in the book-case. These were, a treatise on Baptism,
in which the father of Sir Charles Tupper was severely handled; a work on the Millenium, with a long
prolegomenon; and the *Plan of Salvation*.

The last was posthumous and was edited by the
Master who supplied a preface, written in good style
but, as some might think, overburdened with scriptural proof of his position. The manuscript of this

book was copied by his sister, Mary, and her designation of "amanuensis" seemed to lend great dignity to her task, although it also suggested how far she fell short of authorship. He too was careful to insist upon the subordination of his own function as editor. The proofs of this book, as they came from the printer, were the first I ever saw, and I was even allowed to read them in search of technical errors. The first book I ever owned was *God's Way of Truth*, by a devout man named Scott. It was given by a colporteur as a delicate return for his regular food and lodging in the Master's house over a period of several years. The price, four pence, was printed on the front page, opposite to a silhouette of the author in gown, bands, and wig. A visiting grandaunt professed a liking for the book, and the Master lent it to her. I was desolate, and had a bitter sense of wrong. I used every device of suggestion to have it returned, but knew that a year at least would elapse. It was brought back, and I read in it to this day.

Into the manymansioned house of literature I had entrance by a strange door. There was a book which for a long time successfully concealed itself under the forbidding title, *Reminiscences of Scottish Life and Character*, by Dean Ramsay. But one wet and desolate Sabbath I dragged it into the light, and the day was no longer desolate. The author protests continually that he tells his stories not for their humour but of necessity to illustrate his thesis. I had seen enough of this conventional subterfuge, and knew that he wrote out of the sheer fun that was in his heart. But it was Dean Swift who finally showed me the mystery.

The book was *Gulliver's Travels*. I had been allowed to go on a wagon a distance of four miles to a wharf where a schooner was discharging cedar logs. The journey occupied a summer day, and I read the whole book. The thing was so amazing I could not forbear from mentioning it to the Master. "It is only a satire," he said; and as that did not seem to make the matter any clearer, he added, "a piece of fun about the way people act." So it came to this : literature has something to do with life — and fun.

And next there was *The Complete Works of William Shakespeare* in a tall red single volume. Before I had learned to read so vast a work, an elder brother had told me the plots of all the plays. He made a mystery of his knowledge, until I discovered it was drawn not from the original source but from *Lamb's Tales*. To him it was a profitable mystery, for I would willingly perform small tasks for him, like weeding a flower-bed or picking beans, whilst he stood by and lived idly by his art. I examined the large book for myself, and discovered a new world to be explored.

It was not a point of honour in that family that a child, if questioned, should conceal the wrong doing of another; and Shakespeare could not be read openly on the Sabbath, which was the only day free for so large an enterprise. There lay across the farm "the big hollow," dank from a slow stream and grown with luscious grass. It lay between unfenced fields, and was forbidden to cattle unless they were herded.

Any child who wished to acquire merit could herd a favourite cow on a corner of grass. I formed the large design of taking all three to the big hollow. The result was admirable. Such a flow of milk had never been witnessed. The next Sabbath, I was not only allowed, but encouraged, to repeat the performance, and I brought the Shakespeare with me. With the abundance of water and grass the beasts were soon satisfied, and I lay on the bank with them in glorious ease. That book lasted one whole summer.

The Master's wife had a hatred of any printed thing unless it were printed in Latin or Greek or in algebraic symbols. Of these she had no personal knowledge, but she was certain of their value. She had known boys, who could read Latin and Greek, become ministers, lawyers, doctors, members of parliament; and a familiarity with mathematics was said to be useful to a sea-captain, although her own uncle had crossed the Atlantic all his life without any assistance from that occult science. Her husband's people had followed the way of letters for four hundred years at least, and not one had been compelled to work with his hands.

One important observation she made. If it were all an affair of words, the place to learn of words was in the dictionary, the spelling-book, and the grammar. Her complaint was that those who wrote other books knew nothing; and even if they did know anything serious they could not teach it by writing. One learned by doing and by seeing done. Could a child learn from a book how a square knot was tied or a running bowline made ? — a knot which she had heard from her uncle would hold a bull by the horns or the devil by the tail. Reading was a waste of time, a sign of laziness, a debauching of the mind.

But she was compelled in time to take account of the rising talk about "literature." She went to headquarters and examined Shakespeare for herself. Much of it she found foolish, tedious, stupid, and some of it scandalously coarse. The characters did not interest her. She knew living men whom they resembled, and she preferred the originals. Then she would recite the names of those persons, and amplify the poet's description with treasures hidden in her own memory. Finally, she allowed, the plays might do very well for idle, ignorant people who lived in towns, and knew nothing of life.

In my young eagerness I read to her, 'The cloud capp'd towers, the gorgeous palaces.' "It sounds well," she admitted, and called to mind the case of a Catholic neighbour who wished to call his child Martin Luther, because the name sounded well. If it were a case of clouds, "I could go and look at the clouds for myself." If it were an affair of palaces ... She turned upon me with her own book, and bewildered me with the splendour of Isaiah and the imagination of Ezekiel, Daniel, and the Apocalypse. She would never admit that the Bible was "a religious book." If it were that only she would not have read it. Many years passed before I understood her meaning. One of the two books I brought into the field of war was *The Tempest*. I was not there long before

I gave it to a Belgian woman who was trying to learn English.

Even upon those far intellectual shores the evolutionary movement of the mid-nineteenth century was felt. In the *Montreal Witness* the Master's wife had seen the hairy picture of Charles Darwin, and from that imperfect evidence she thought there might be something in his doctrine in so far at most as he himself was concerned. In the wake of that movement came the new apothesis of "science." For that she had ready the words of the Apostle, "Science falsely so-called." The new word in every amateur scientific mouth was "truth." To her the truth was one with the way and the life. The "scientists" were satisfied when they had given a Latin name to a thing, and assigned it to a category which often turned out to be the wrong one. She did not think the perception of a strawberry was increased by calling it *fragaria vesca*; a "grey-bird" was quite as true as a *junco*.

Of one thing she was convinced : whatever the ascent of men and women might be, their descent to the status of the beast was inevitable, unless they minded themselves. To avoid this degradation there were certain conventions of which the first was modesty. The sense of shame for protection of the mind was powerful as the sense of pain for protection of the body. The absence of that sense was to her the distinguishing mark of the beast; and for a woman so marked she had one final word of categorical designation.

This practice of modesty was carried to such a

point that a woman would not appear in public without a mantle or other garment that would effectively conceal any indication of her feminity. A child was taught "to look the other way" from things he should not see. Words too specific of certain functions were eschewed, and even those words were avoided which called up any image that was unpleasant. "Plain speaking" about quite obvious things was the mark of a coarse and disgusting mind. There were many conventions of speech in which a word or a phrase more agreeable or less offensive, yet none the less accurate, was substituted for one more coarsely expressive of what was meant. Silence was decent; reticence was not hypocrisy. Exuberance of language was strictly checked. Sayings by young persons, that were commonly considered smart and bright, were proscribed as merely impudent. There was a further ban upon words good enough in themselves but corrupted by association with unpleasant ideas.

There was one absolute rule : anything that occurred in the house was not to be disclosed; anything unworthy heard outside was not to be brought in. If a child were pressed by a curious neighbour upon a doubtful matter, he was to answer, "I cannot say," leaving it to be impartially surmised whether his reticence was due to lack of knowledge or to an injunction not to say.

Reticence and secrecy was with her a convention. Her children were fond of pressing her with questions, and discovering actions that were quite obvious, as mischievous persons like to spoil a performance

on the stage. To convict her of Sabbath breaking was
an easy device. She would not allow bread to be
baked on the holy day; although a few biscuits might
be put in the pan. Nor would she permit clothes to
be washed, although she herself might "rinse out a
few things and hang them on a hedge in the sun."
To the suggestion that the eye of God was upon the
most secluded hedge her answer was; that she was
not afraid of God, but was afraid of the neighbour's
talk.

Of only one other force was she afraid. Thunder
and lightning left her prostrate. Whilst the storm
lasted, her terror was extreme. Doors were shut,
blinds drawn, but the dark stillness only increased the
sense of fear. A child soon learned that thunder was
the voice of the very angry God, and the sky riven to
afford a glimpse into a still more angry hell. The
grandmother stood in the door entranced by the
spectacle, her face glowing with delight.

The fir tree is the tree of that country. A pest fell
upon the firs, and in time destroyed the surrounding
woods. The house was then under observation.
Young trees were planted. After twenty years the
protecting screen was complete again, and the Master's wife lived and died content in security: Then a
friendly neighbour lamented that she was herself
isolated in her old age. I cut away enough of the trees
to allow an unobstructed view of the place and its
new activities, in which she still finds some strange
interest.

X

THE ECONOMY OF THE HOUSE

THE spirit of economy was accepted by the household for two reasons. It permitted a lavish display in the presence of strangers by which the prestige of the family was enlarged; it provided the occasional feasts in which all shared. The mother's theory of health was that a child should be kept on the verge of hunger, and occasionally allowed a surfeit of food. Yet it was her boast that no cupboard was ever locked.

A boy who did not eat his porridge at breakfast was either not hungry or he was sick. To provide any other form of food for him would be useless in the one case and harmful in the other. A child did not expect praise for the feat of finishing what was set before him. If he failed in the task, that was proof that he had received too much, and the error would be corrected on future occasions.

It is the simplest dishes that demand the utmost refinement in the art of cookery. To bake a potato, to boil a herring, to broil a trout, to bake bread, to roast a goose, to brown an apple, to make porridge — that is the final test of skill. The minister of another parish for thirty-five years was in the habit of making his porridge with his own hand. His eldest daughter, although she had studied the ceremonial all that time

and finally assumed the office, confessed before she
died that only once had she attained to complete
perfection. But in the making of porridge there is no
law. Four women visitors would be in the kitchen
at the same moment, each one preparing the
confection to suit her husband's taste which she had
studied so long. But refinement in the art of porridge
may be pushed beyond the point of luxury and
become a vice.

The Master's wife, towards the end of her days,
would expel intruders from the kitchen, and perform
a feat of cookery as a proof that her power and
authority was not abated. Those strange servants
who of later years accompanied her children and her
children's children in their summer irruptions were
a sore trial to her. They interfered with her liberty.
She had only two perfectly happy days, the day they
came and the day they went.

For strangers there must be a full table, and she
never could reconcile herself to the modern practice
of removing all food after each course. She thought
the board looked poor, mean, and bare, without
so much as a cruet-stand. On the seldom occasion
of a return visit by her, she demanded the full ceremonial of hospitality. A cup of tea and a few biscuits
sliding about a plate would not do. All work must
be suspended and other social obligations carefully
concealed. She held it as an especial grievance if any
one who entered her house refused to eat and drink.
The refusal was a mark of obstinancy or truculence
of mind, possibly even a sign of suspicion that there

was a lack of food. Only once was she defied, and that by her own uncle. In spite of his reiterated, "No, Catherine, no," she proceeded with the preparation of the meal; but with equal firmness he removed the kettle from the fire, carried it outside and deposited it in the snow.

But cookery and eating was not the whole of life. For men it had some importance; for women little. "I suppose you will not be setting the table, since Himself is away," an old servant said one day the Master had gone to town. "A cup of tea in her hand" was considered enough for a woman. The Master's wife was fond of tea. Her taste for tea was keen as the taste of a connoisseur for wine. "The worst cup of tea she ever had in her life," was the last word in criticism of a housekeeper. Upon her arrival after a railway journey, she was asked if she had been well served with tea at Moncton. "No," she said.

"Did you speak to the woman ? "

"I did."

"What did you say to her ? "

"I told her I had been keeping house for sixty-three years, and had never given any one so bad a cup of tea — to say nothing of being charged ten cents for it."

In the early days tea-drinking was always a luxury, sometimes it too was a vice. On either ground it was a subject of conflict between men and their wives. A cautious woman would brew her tea on the coals of the hearth, and then sweep away the ashes so that the imprint of the tea-pot would not remain as ev-

idence of her crime. When the open-hearth was replaced by the stove, she would thrust the pot in the
oven at the first sign of danger. One woman about
to be caught in the act threw "pot and all" out at the
open window. In summer a woman could keep herself supplied with tea by the surreptitious exchange
of a few eggs, but in winter she would be hard pressed.

One Mrs. McTavish in her desperation took a
sheaf of timothy, and beat out the seed. She concealed the hay by feeding it to the cattle, and carried
the precious seed to the woods where she sifted it on
the snow. In exchange for the seed she bought a
little tea. But in the spring the man discovered
the chaff in the woods. The Master's wife rarely
reprehended the conduct of men, but this one she
thought "too strict."

Even a male child by reason of his masculinity
was regarded as a potential enemy. One of the younger generation received much praise from a very old
woman who had memories of stricter days. "He is a
mannerly boy," she said. "He will not be enquiring
into the business of women." In time of great need,
a myrtle plant that grew wild in the woods was a
means of comfort to those emigrants from Scotland.

Coffee was not used. There was a coffee-mill in
the house, but it was only brought into service when
a grand-uncle returned from a voyage with some of
the green unroasted berries, or to grind parched
barley as a substitute for tea as a drink. For children
there was neither tea nor coffee; their drink was milk,
or in winter, milk with hot water. My first experience

of coffee was in the Minister's house. His wife was a foreign woman, that is, from Nova Scotia. She gave me a cup; and the strange exotic flavour and fragrance gave entrance into a new world.

Sugar was scarce. It was bought by the pound. Two pounds was the complement of one pound of tea. It came from the Barbados in brown shining crystals. The sugar loaf had almost disappeared, and its place was taken by broken lumps. Much later, the now familiar cubes made their appearance. They were placed in two layers in a flat paper box. I saw an open box on the shop counter. Worse still, the box was only partly filled, and a single lump could not be missed. The merchant was absent for a moment. The kingdom of this world was before me. It was a frightful moment. Ever since, I have understood the mind of a criminal, the one who yields, and the one who resists.

The brilliant brown Barbados sugar was in time replaced by the dirty yellow product of the beet. The mother always contended that there was no sweetness in it, and the now familiar granulated sugar became the habit. This debasement of all manufactured goods extended in her mind to natural products as well, even to mushrooms. When the house-fly became troublesome, she would go to the woods for mushrooms, and make a solution with syrup for their destruction. All yellow mushrooms were understood to be poisonous; but on one occasion they had no effect on the flies. From this experience she was convinced that "even mushrooms were no good any more." By mistake she had gathered the *chanterelle*, which with its fragrant fruity smell is safe and delicious for men as well as flies. The very newspapers were so badly made, they would not serve to light the fire.

The standard "sweetening" was molasses. It was brought by sea from the West Indies in puncheons, and was sold by the gallon. When the puncheon was empty, it also was sold. With the head removed it served to hold rain water, seed wheat, or any precious commodity. Sawn in two, it would make large tubs which were admirable as watering troughs or even for scalding a pig. But the puncheon was always sold unopened, and it contained a residue of coarse moist sugar, more or less in quantity. What that amount might be was a subject of exciting speculation. It was the one chance in the year of obtaining something for nothing.

With the purchase of soap all need of saving fat was at an end. In former times fat was a precious commodity; it became so again in the stress of war. Of all forms of fat, butter was the most precious. To provide in the short summer a supply for the winter demanded resolution against children clamouring for milk and cream. In later years when it became the habit of some to send the milk to the factory, children were stinted; they were deprived of the by-products, the skimmed milk, the buttermilk, the whey, the curds; and the Master's wife always protested that she could discover the families that sent milk to the factory by the starved look of their children.

Butter was so precious that a woman would take a lock of wool and wipe every knife and plate. The saturated morsel so saved would then serve as oil for the wool in process of carding.

The making of soap in the house demanded that the coarser kinds of grease be saved for a whole year, since soap could only be made in the spring. That was the time when potash was at hand. In the summer soft wood was burned. In the winter the ashes from the hard wood, which alone yield potash, were saved in a barrel, and in the spring, the alkali was leached out with water. In the meantime, the factories were at their insidious work, and supplied "concentrated lye." The ashes were wasted. With the failure of domestic economy, the Master's wife was quite sure that civilization itself would be destroyed.

She always made the clothes for the younger children; resort to the tailor was a sign of approaching manhood. But approach to the tailor was through a preliminary stage when he merely measured the boy and cut the cloth, leaving the garments to be made at home. To secure a perfect fit he spread the cloth on the floor; the boy lay down upon the cloth, and the tailor cut to his shape. His charge for the operation was twelve cents, and it was not to be incurred lightly. The first complete experience of the tailor was not encouraging. An elder brother was involved in the transaction, and the tailor attached legs of different lengths to each pair of trousers.

This tailor, Sandy Martin, was lame of a leg. Possibly on that account he considered trousers with legs of unequal length to be the normal. His son, Donald, who succeeded him in the trade, had a precisely similar defect, due doubtless to inherited tubercular disease of the hip-joint. It was the custom for a stallion horse to be travelled through the country in the springtime, and his enormous hoofprints on the road were a matter of wonder. A new Kentucky stallion was due to arrive. He had been imported at a cheap price, as he was lame from an accident to his fetlock. A boy was sent to the "stand" to inspect the horse, and the report he brought back was quite adverse. But the father, being well instructed in the evolutionary doctrine that acquired defects are not transmitted, declared the lameness to be no bar to service. His son was not convinced, and in opposition cited the sequential lameness of the tailors, Sandy Martin and Donald.

This spirit of economy, when thoroughly set, can never be eradicated. It explains the "petty meanness" of many rich men. One rich man always referred to his fortune as the poor few shillings he had managed to save from his hard earnings. Another would scrutinize the bill of fare at an elaborate hotel or exclusive club for the least expensive item, even whilst he craved some unseasonable dainty. He strove by calculated extravagance to break the useless habit; but his misery was so extreme that he abandoned the attempt. Rich men should be judged less hardly.

To live is an art. The material at hand must be subdued to the purposes of life. The essence of art is economy, that nothing be wasted. To write as Mr.

Kipling writes, to draw as Mr. *Punch* draws, to paint as Ver Meer paints, to live as we lived, is merely to practice economy, without waste, without meanness. The writer who wastes words becomes a journalist; the draughtsman who wastes lines, a fumbler searching blindly; the painter wasting colour a striver after impressions he has never felt.

Art is management of words, sound, line, colour. Economy is the highest art in the management of a house. In life, as in every work of art, this note must be true and dominant over all else. Life and art become mean, poor, and debased when they lack control by some principle of unity. Life is never mean when it is lived at the proper level; and there is no poverty where there is no pretence. The soldier in his hut, the priest in his cubicle, the family in the cottage — none of these are poor so long as they live in subordination to their essential idea. They are artists seeking to express themselves with not how much but with how little. They become comic and contemptible only when they strive to live above their need and beyond their means. The comedian has discovered this principle, and made it his own. The pretender is the subject of his wit, and he makes the rich man practising parsimony as comic as the poor man who apes the habits of those beyond his class.

With the Master's wife, economy was an art, but she was slow to recognize that the factory had broken down the well-established fabric of domestic life. The apparent cheapness of articles which began to fill the shops, and the ease with which they could be obtain-

ed, destroyed the hardy spirit of economy; and when
the old order was broken at one point it failed in all.
Without the sanded floor there was now no means
of restoring a rusty needle; a new one must be bought.
When she found her needle rusted, she would place it
on the floor, and roll it under her foot at an incredible
speed. In a moment the needle was polished bright.
This is an allegory.

When a manufactured article was done with, it
was finished. A boot that leaked was fit only for the
fire. An article made in the house had several successive lives. A piece of cloth would serve in turn for
a man's coat, and a child's jacket. Cut in smaller
pieces, it could be sewn into a quilt. Cut into strips
these could be hooked or woven into mats, which
would migrate from parlour to kitchen, and finally
to the barns. The Master's wife could trace the history of a shred of cloth backwards through its various
forms for sixty years. And these forms from coat to
mat were assumed without expense, since the change
was made in the spare time. One match a day was
the proper ration. In her childhood there were no
matches. If the fire went out it was laboriously kind-
led with flint and steel, or a brand was borrowed
from the house of a more provident neighbour. It is
no wonder that diligent and thrifty people became
rich.

She had little faith in the laudable attempts to
revive those old industries, arts, and handicrafts. The
mind of the young people had changed. And yet she
looked with delight upon any sign of revival — it

might be a web of cloth, a tanned sheep-skin, a set of harness made from native leather, a spinning wheel or a loom brought into the house. She was glad there was something permanent to be left behind her. Donald Gordon had made her first wheel, and it was yet in occasional use as she taught a grandchild to spin. This wheel was seventy years old, but the maker was yet alive. He made a new one so like the old she could scarcely distinguish between them. He averred this was the last wheel he would ever make, which was extremely probable, as he was then in his ninety-fourth year. He must now be dead or, if living, a very old man; and there is none now left to make a wheel. The old wheel is yet in daily use on the Pacific, not the Atlantic coast.

Into this world of industry came the facile and fatal aniline dyes. The Master's wife would have none of them. When she was old, I made a foolish attempt to revive those arts. Indigo, which I supplied, was the foundation of the colour scheme. When the first web of "draft-weaving" arrived, she unrolled it on the floor to the length of ten yards. She knelt down and examined the cloth thread by thread. "The woman has used aniline blue, not indigo," she declared. I protested, but she said nothing. Next day she announced that she was going by herself to a shop some miles away on business of her own. This shop was in the district where the cloth was made. What her business was no one could surmise, and she was "not in the habit of being questioned." She brought back the proof. She enquired of the man if he had any aniline blue dye. He had none at the moment, as he had just sold it all. Being asked for an opinion of its quality, he assured her it was excellent; and being pressed for further proof, he quoted as final authority the name of the very woman who had woven the cloth.

XI

THE WRITTEN WORD

SOLDIERS, sailors, farmers, school-boys, women who have borne children, all who come in close contact with the frightful forces of the world, have the same contempt for talk and written words. The great writers — even Plato himself — understood the secondary nature of their occupation. I was once in company with Mr. Kipling, when we were joined by a sailor fresh from the sea. Mr. Kipling disclosed a sudden change of demeanour, a certain deference, and by that I learned how subtle and profound a perception he had. His own boy once implored him to stop writing, or at least not to publish, during term-time.

On a sea-voyage I was invited by the captain to occupy a handsome cabin next to his own. He had come from Pictou. In my simplicity I gave him a book by a writer, Joseph Conrad, who at the time was reputed to be a master in tales of the sea. The book was *The Typhoon*. On the return voyage, the captain was silent about the book. I asked him if he had read it. He confessed with a tinge of shame "that he had read a piece of it." He did not appear to think much of it — "The man only wrote down what someone else had done." This sailor had made his headquarters in New York for thirty years. I praised his residence. "It was a great city," he allowed "but what do you think of a place," he asked, "where a man could not buy as much as a red turnip, or barley meal, or a salted herring?" These to him were long realities.

I knew a man again who had visited Egypt. He had seen "the slow river," "the piles of stones," "the image of a creature half buried in the sand, no better than school-boys could make with snow"; but he had complete and living knowledge of the Church of Scotland on the Shiria Abbas, near the "level crossing," and of the doctrine he heard preached therein.

Sailors will remember foreign ports in terms of the liquor they obtained. I was once given a description of Palermo by a sea-faring man, from which I inferred that Palermo was a cool corner, comfortable with rush bottomed chairs, tables laden with long bread and pickled pig's feet; familiar with hens and cats that would solicit a crumb or a bite; with rows of casks extending into the dark distance, "as high as a man's head, from which if one drank enough he would sleep for fourteen hours and wake up feeling all the better for it." Athens pleased him best of all; for there "one could sit on the sidewalk, and drink a liquor as sweet as wine and strong as brandy with a fragrant taste of resin, and all for two-pence the large glass." Those who write should think of these things.

A man, so thought the Master's wife, could see only through his own eyes; he could see only what interested him, and what he saw might not be of the least interest to others; he could not explain what he saw, unless his readers had a somewhat similar experience. This restricted or destroyed, the value of reading. After I had made a journey that took me through the Red Sea in August, I told her of Arabs, and heat, and scarlet flamingos. She was unmoved. Had I told her of a division of the water and chariots lying on the bottom, she would have been interested in the narrative although she would not have believed in the discovery.

It was by wisdom, not from insensibility, that she read no books. Her life was full and rich by living a full and rich life. Her experience could not be increased by reading what others said they felt. She much preferred to enlarge her own experience by looking upon sunset and sunrise, by watching the seasons come and go, by walking in the woods and fields, by observing plants and animals, by conversing with neighbours in their diverse mental moods. For all else she had neither time nor desire. Reading was mere idle curiosity. One could not understand another way of life unless one lived it. If it were a question of entertainment, she was most entertained in her own world; and had no desire to seek entrance into the unreal world of the word makers. Besides, the heavenly city was always within the compass of her vision.

Her opinion was that if a person read many books they would neutralize one another, and the reader would not be led astray by any one. A single book was a false guide. Of the alternatives she thought the better way was to leave them alone; it saved time for more important labour. Once embarked on the course of reading, it was equally perilous to stop, to continue, or to turn back.

Her censorship of books was strict, and she "never could understand how they came into the house." If a boy were found with a book, he was asked to read aloud — and any detached passage from a story always sounds foolish. By such means he was for the moment convicted if not convinced of his folly. One day — and to make matters worse it was the Sabbath — I was discovered in the act of reading *Adam Bede,* a book by a writer known as George Eliot.

To make matters still worse, she had heard that there was something ambiguous about this author — neither man nor woman, neither married nor single. I was instantly put to the usual test. I shut the book, but an exculpatory passage leaped into my mind, and by the providence of God, the book opened at the spot. I read the sentences with an emotion arising out of my assurance of escape; but to her the inspiration seemed to be inherent in the sentiments that were being read. It was *Dinah's* invocation : "Saviour of sinners ! when a poor woman, laden with sins, went out to the well to draw water, she found Thee sitting at the well. She knew Thee not; she had not sought Thee. But Thou didst speak to her. Thou didst teach her. Jesus, Thou art in the midst of us. Lord, Thou art with Thy people still."

I had "skipped" this part. Now there was fresh interest. The kind of book she hated most was "religious reading." The Master found virtue in the practice of reading aloud, possibly because he read so well, and enjoyed his own performance, as all artists do. When he suspected inattention he would suddenly demand of some child, "Last word ? "

I finished *Dinah's* prayer, and plunged into her sermon. I read page after page, skilfully omitting the bits of narrative with which the author had lightened the theme. When I was about to emerge upon secular ground, I demanded with some asperity, "Last word?" Her word was, "There seems to be no harm in the book; put it away; it sounds like a Methodist book." She did not like to see a boy even reading the Bible at random; it was unnatural; she suspected insincerity — or worse. To learn by rote a set piece was different; the task had at least a disciplinary value.

This dislike of reading and hatred of sentimentality was a trial to the Master. The defect he attributed to "the Smiths." When he was young and frequenting their house, he proposed for their entertainment to read in a book he had brought. The eldest of the uncles before giving assent required that he be shown the book, so that he might estimate the length of the piece proposed to be read.

The grandmother was an inveterate reader of newspapers, magazines, and other romances — everything but the Bible; and all in the community who had books brought them to her. We watched for them as a jackdaw watches for a shining thing. On the other hand, she too exercised a prescriptive censorship over our books; but it was observed that she would read the book from the beginning to end before passing judgement which, however, was always favourable. The Master on occasion would read an article in *Blackwood's*; but he always marked it "read," in case by error he should read it again. If the winter days were short, the nights were long; but they were not dull either. The Master would read aloud, but the practice was not encouraged by his wife; it kept the children from their more profitable books. On rare occasions neighbours were invited, when the evening was enlivened by secular songs, trivial games, and a bounteous supper.

Whatever benefit there may be in pictures was denied to us. There were a few on the walls, but we did not understand them. Trees came through the roof of a house; and the house cast a shadow in two directions; the shadow itself was solid as a bank of snow, as in some more modern pictures. Three things I did not understand : a man wearing a monocle, a man with a crushed opera hat, a man with the corners of his coat cut away. Not even Tenniel's drawings in *Punch* could make them real. The pictures on the modern screen are not more real to the devotees of that form of art; they are too ignorant of the objects depicted. On the wall was a picture of the first Orangeman, which was removed if any of the Catholic neighbours appeared. But a highly censorious Elder found scriptural warrant against all pictures. "You will turn them to the wall, Catherine," he said, as he entered the bedroom. They were highly fanciful representations of the seasons in the guise of young maidens.

"They put me in mind of spring and summer," she protested.

"Thou shalt not make unto thee any graven image, or any likeness of any thing that is in heaven above, or that is in the earth beneath," he quoted with awful authority.

"These pictures are not like any thing in heaven or earth," she argued.

"You will turn them to the wall. They will be following me with their eyes."

"Close your eyes, and they will not trouble you."

"They disturb my mind even in the dark."

"Let your mind dwell upon better things."

"You will ever have the last word, Woman."

"And my last word is, 'Good night.' " She closed the door upon the angry old man; but there was anger in her own heart.

Let parents beware of the intelligence of a child, even when he is asleep. "That old man is no better than the Apostle Paul," she said, when she rejoined the Master. Then ensued an obscure conversation, dimly apprehended; she protesting against the narrowness of the life into which she had come; whilst he appeased and explained, and even confessed a lack of complete faith in the austere practice he had made his own.

"I never believed the heathen were so bad as Paul makes out," she said; and added, as if a great light had dawned upon her, "I think they must have been something like my own people; and I like them better than that old man in the spare room." Her reserve had broken down. In low but passionate words, she protested that she would rather live amongst the Catholics with their pictures and images than with those who could see no beauty or meaning in the earthly creation.

"Do not let the children hear you say that," he implored.

"The children know it already. It is fun they make of him; and they will end by making fun of you, and of the Apostle as well."

"Do not let them hear that dangerous doctrine," he implored again with a distress that was pitiful; but one child had already heard.

The first public attempt at dramatic art was not a success. The play was good, the stage was complete with all conventions, including a trap-door, a flash of light, and a smell of sulphur. The female part was taken by a young man so accurately dressed in his sister's clothes that he was mistaken for her. The play demanded that he should kiss his husband. This realism in public was too much. There was open protest. The performance was not repeated.

The Master's wife had a daughter with an exquisite gift in mimicry and disguise. In the dusk of a winter evening, she would array herself like an old woman, and enter the house, where the Master's wife would be left conveniently alone for the performance. After an affectionate greeting and protest-

ation of gratitude, she would announce that she had
come to spend the remainder of the winter. Then
would follow a moving account of her poverty and
the harshness of her own people, in contrast with the
atmosphere in which she proposed to live. The Master's wife met or evaded every argument, and to post-
pone judgement proposed a cup of tea. When she returned with a well-set tray, the woman was gone.
"My mind must be failing," she announced; but not
a word of the incident upon which her conclusion
was based.

The Master's wife never applied a pen to paper
after she left school. No letter of hers exists. And
yet she wrote a script as fine and free and firm as
if it were engraved on metal. Her exercise books,
now bound in morocco, attest to the truth of this.
In early life there was no occasion to write; her friends
and relations were round about her. In later years,
when her children were scattered, they knew, she
implied, what was in her heart; but she received their
letters with great joy. She knew our trials and cares.
She never asked us to return even for a visit : "You
will come home when you can, without my writing
to you."

She had a sure judgement of persons who came
from that larger world to enter into her house. One
went away without having said good-bye to her; "that
had never happened before." The one she loved best
was the "Old Gentleman." He had the sympathy
that enabled him to discover her instincts, thoughts,
and prejudices; he had the literary skill — and that is

all literature amounts to — by which he could translate them into a language of which she was incapable; he was a formidable ally in argument, and could say for her things she had been longing to say all her life, but could not.

Amongst her treasures was found a letter from this "Old Gentleman," which she had never shewn to anyone. It is dated February 8th, 1913 : "I never before participated in so intelligent, seemly, kind, racy, and almost devotional discussion of a bottle as that in which the Faculty and myself honoured yours last night. You have reason to be happy in your sons. They know the courtesies befitting to guests, and they approach and proceed in the pleasant exercise of drinking as with a sense of something closely resembling worship of the Omnipotent who has endowed man with power to distil and preserve in glass the 'good creature of God.' Some fine day or week, when leisure arrives to me, if ever it will in the hot race for bread, I shall carefully indite an account of last evening, possibly in verse, though my handling in that medium can never do justice to my delight in remembering the fine and subtle elements of the occasion. I hope the boys enjoyed it as I did, and that they told you, as your proxy in administering hospitality, that I behaved appropriately. How fond your children are of one another. What a pity to die from such a world."

She loved her children. In the words of Richard Rolle, addressed to the Cistercian anchoress of Hampole : If thou wilt ask, how good is he or she, ask how much he or she loves. And that love was bestowed inversely to the strength of the recipient. But her faintest criticism of any one was changed to eulogy by the slightest sign of agreement with that comment. Even praise of any one was resented, unless it were applied equally to all. It was a pretty game, eliciting these various moods, by affecting to blame or praise one for his folly, and another for his merit.

In reply to this letter, she sent a verbal message, that in her family they had always observed the ritual established in the book of Esther : The drinking was according to the law; none did compel; each man drank according to his own pleasure.

It was not long before the eve of War when this same Old Gentleman was sending verse to her, but it was verse of a different kind. In the last stanza she found much comfort :

Spoke then our student-soldier strong of soul,
    Though every phantom of the earth or cloud,
    With sun and moon and all the starry crowd
Move equal on in ignorance of the goal,
Of meaning of the universal whole
    Which beareth onward orbs and empires proud,
    Alike to endure whatever Fate allowed
By that Unknowable which wields control;
    Yet Man hath liberty to mend his plight
    By heeding honour's inmost sacred calls,
    Which, if obeyed, his soul ascendeth free,
    Or, if denied, it sinketh as a thrall's.
    Choose we this hour to rise. And straightway he
Knelt meek, and silent vowed him to the fight.

XII

THE TWO RACES

It is not without reason men say the best English in the world is spoken in Inverness. By continual use a language becomes debased; rubbed and worn by ease and familiarity. When it is learned afresh, the old quality is restored as in new minted coins. By continual attention in the process of learning, the original and essential virtue of words is discovered; and they seem so precious they are used with discrimination and care. The taste and flavour of the strange speech is imported into the new, which is then freshened and enriched as an old and sodden fruit by a graft from the wild. But the speech must be strange, for an allied dialect is only a means of further debasement; the English and the Gaelic were strange enough the one to the other. To yield any benefit the new language must be learned not from those speaking the current jargon but from the pure source of literature.

The grandmother learned English by following in the English Bible the words as they were read in the Gaelic at family worship, and that process of education was fairly continuous. Her husband spoke an educated English, and she learned from him. The Master used the Gaelic as his first language, but he never proceeded very far, and at an early age forgot

much by disuse, although to the end he could exercise
the gift of prayer in that tongue. He retained the
merest flavour of the Highland accent, and spoke
English with respect and unconscious care, with ease
and fluency as if he had known no other. By contrast,
the speech of his mother seemed somewhat archaic
to us in our new perfection, and we came to be known
as "the English-speaking." The illiteracy of the English settlements was a source of amusement, a cause
of derision to us; and we rather resented the designation. A professor of English by whom I was being
examined put to me the problem of "but," used in
the sense of without, as in "touch not a cat but a
glove," and cited as a clue "but and ben" applied to
a two-roomed house. He professed astonishment at
my unfamiliarity with Scottish usage. He was still
more astonished when I protested that, being Highland, I spoke only English and knew nothing of the
jargon of the Lowlands.

In that community, surnames fell into disuse.
They were so few that they were useless for purpose
of definition. Trades were substituted — joiner, tail-
or, shoemaker, mason, rigger, doctor. A man who
lived in a stone house became Stonehouse; if he lived
at the head of a harbour, Kinlock. Personal appearance was employed, and a family would be known as
Ruadh, Gairbh, Bàn, Dubh, according as an ancestor
was red, hairy, white, or black. At times there was
a touch of the comic or even of malice in these design-
ations. A family whose ancestor was notorious for
hard work became known as Beaver; another had

suffered from small-pox, and he was known as *Breac*, the spotted one, which is also the word for trout; and that name transformed into Spreck is still used to designate his family.

The method most commonly employed was to append to the name of a person the first name of his father. In four generations a man would therefore acquire four names, and when they were mentioned it was well understood who he was, for his great-grandfather also was specified. It was a breach of decorum to employ these devices in personal address. In such cases a man must receive his clan name — if one could remember what it was.

The language of the community was Gaelic. Many of the old people spoke no other; all the young "had the English," but they spoke it with peculiar accent, tone, and expression. English was considered to be merely a translation from the Gaelic, and the wonder was, since it was thought necessary to translate it at all, why the work should have been so badly done. The poverty of the English was well known — the lack of cases and genders : "It had the same word for everything, and a boy was the same as a girl." The analogy of any other plague or pest helped to elucidate "the great progress of English in the world"; for it was well known that whole communities had long since ceased speaking Gaelic. In England and in "the States" this ignorance was said to be universal.

It was also their belief that all rational and articulate persons must have the Gaelic, but may conceal it through fear, pride, or other unworthy motive.

The "French gentleman" who once visited Orwell learned the single exclamation, *Na chunnaic mi,* What I saw! It remained in his universal mind. Long afterwards he was on a voyage in a private yacht to tropic seas. There was a Highland steward. The artist, in simulated excitement, and muttering his solitary phrase, contrived to meet the steward suddenly around the corner of the house. With the reticence of his race, the steward made as if he did not hear; he had surprised a man in the betrayal of his own secret; but thenceforth he was a brother to him.

Where two languages meet there is much that is amusing. A boy who spoke only English was sent to carry to an old woman who spoke Gaelic alone the message that her daughter was dead. The distance was seven miles; the day was wet. As he walked he had a pleasant excitement over the importance of his task and some interest in the emotion the woman would display. But she heard the message calmly and only repeated *fliuch, fliuch.* On the way home he kept saying to himself *fliuch, fliuch.* He asked his mother what the word meant. She told him that *fliuch* was the Gaelic for *it is a wet day.* The old woman had understood not a word of the message.

A common subject of merriment was the ignorance of English-speaking people, and the mistakes they made. These mistakes were always comic or absurd; sometimes they were obscene as well. It was a diversion having them pronounce words of peculiar difficulty. The test word was *laogh,* which means a calf. It looks easy but it is not pronounced at all as one would suppose. A diversion for the evening was singing Gaelic songs, or rather a song; for all songs seemed to be one song. It was not until I heard Mairi Matheson at the Aeolian Hall in Bond Street that I discovered how large the repertory is. That celebrated Czech, Karel Capek, was similarly deceived by the apparent unity and simplicity of Highland music; he was equally deceived by the apparent simplicity of the spelling. During his residence in the Isle of Skye he thought he heard only one song :

> *Tha tighinn fodham, fodham, fodham,*
> *Tha tighinn fodham, fodham, fodham,*
> *Tha tighinn fodham, fodham, fodham,*
> *Tha tighinn fodham, eirich.*

This is merely the chorus of the fine old Jacobite song, "The time has come for me to rise."

Every year the surplus young men and women migrated to Boston as freely as the sea-birds. There they found friends, work and money; but when they came home it was observed that they had exchanged the more fashionable American speech for the tender Highland cadence of their English that had been so hardly won.

XIII

THE WORLD OF RELIGION

THAT community of Highlanders, cast adrift in a new world, free from family tradition and loyalty to the clan, would have fallen into savagery had it not been ennobled by the spirit of religion. There were, of course, in the older settlements some places of formal worship, and the Catholic Church had made ample provision for her own. Suddenly an apostle appeared, and disclosed religion as the dominant passion of life. His name was Donald MacDonald, a duly ordained minister of the Church of Scotland.

This man arrived in the year 1828; he died in 1867. For forty years he went about amongst the people; he blazed his way through the forest; he swam rivers in summer; in winter he passed by the ice. In that lifetime he saw those isolated settlers become compact in rich, prosperous, and civilized communities. He preached to the ignorant; he strengthened the faithful; he rebuked the wicked, comforted the weak, and healed the sick by the power that animated himself. Before he died, he saw a church with fourteen places of worship, eight thousand members and adherents. The Master early came under his influence. From him the older children had baptism.

Amongst simple people the first manifestations

of religion are always the same, and they are always violent. Amongst the Christians of the first century, the experience was not different. "What meaneth this ? " men said on the Day of Pentecost. For those who are curious as to what it really does mean there is a very specific account which is easily accessible. It meant that the power of God was made manifest upon the people.

Gaelic was the language of the church where we worshipped. For three Sabbaths in the month the only service was a prayer-meeting conducted by the elders; of these only two were competent "to go on" in English. The psalm was read and sung, the chapter read, and the prayer delivered in Gaelic. The only concession was the announcement in English of the number of the psalm and the place of the chapter. The minister on his day held a stricter balance. Psalms and chapters were equally favoured in both tongues. He would open up the subject of the sermon in English for the space of an hour; but when he came to the deeper parts, and the resources of the English tongue were exhausted, he would "take to the Gaelic" for the remaining hour.

One Sabbath morning, an elder took the books, and began to read, as the custom was, where the book opened. When he came to the familiar verse, "Now Barabbas was a robber," remembrance was upon him of the previous day, when he was compelled to make a journey of twenty miles on foot to the town on business with a lawyer about his mortgage. For the word in the text, *robair,* unconsciously he substituted *fear-lagha*, which is the Gaelic word for lawyer; and everyone knew what was in his mind.

These psalms were sung with great fervour, possibly with more interest in the sound than in the sense. Each line was boldly declaimed by a precentor. He pitched the tune. The elders made the attack and the congregation fell in as they could. As only six tunes were used, all much alike, no one was ever far astray. That spiritual experience which justified a man for ordination to the eldership was held to confer upon him a skill in music sufficient for his function. When the precentor and the men found the "tune get too high for them," the women would bear it aloft into a region of amazing shrillness and beauty.

One day the precentor was disturbed in his ecstasy by the sight of a dog; and as it was not seemly "that the children's bread be cast before dogs," he called to his son, whose name was Archie, to expel the dog. But he neglected to put off the quality of precentor, and the command to his son was uttered in the full rhythm and ceremonial of his office : *Archie, eirich, agus curamach an cu*. The whole congregation in unison reinforced the injunction as if it were a divine command contained in the psalm.

The tunes were six in number. They were chosen according to the mood of the psalm : Coleshill — apprehension; Bangor — intercession; Walsall — confession; St. David — acknowledgement; a tune unnamed — thanksgiving; Martyrdom — praise. The first three were in the minor mode and Gregorian style; the last were major, and all for common metre.

Coleshill

As written

Barton's Psalms — 1706

As sung

Solennemente e sostenuto

SALM CXLI

Seanair

Omit in 1st verse *

O Dhia a ta mi 'g éigheach riut

Tional

1st verse   Other verses

O Dhia a ta mi 'g éigheach riut

Seanair

Omit in 1st verse

dean deifir Thu-qam féin

Tional

dean dei-fir Thu-qam féin

Seanair

Is tabhair éisdeachd fòs do m'ghuth

Tional

Is tabh-air éis-deachd fòs do m'ghuth

Seanair

Tràth ghlaodham riut a'm'fheum

Tional

tràth ghlaodh-am riut a'm' fheum

* A verse consists of four lines

The first of these, Coleshill, will serve as an example of the first mood. It is written in A-minor, not to the modern, but to the Gregorian scale; the minor seventh being used instead of the major seventh, and the triad of the second last chord the fourth instead of the fifth.

The printed paradigm shows in the two first staves the tune as written in Barton's *Psalms*, 1706, and followed in modern hymn-books. The remainder indicates the development as practised in the church at Orwell, for the 141st psalm in Gaelic, by precentor and congregation. *Seanair* means elder : *tional* — meeting; verse — four lines.

In the fully harmonized score, from which the air alone is copied, the chords must all be common chords without dissonances. The score was harmonized not by the Master but by Gregor Ketiladze of Tiflis, whose native perception was increased by a visit to the Island. When it was played on the organ, as a voluntary, in a large church, objection was taken on two grounds; that the music was too "classical," that it was too suggestive of the Catholic Church. The musical elements in these six tunes were being elaborated into an opera by Max Heinrich, but death untimely intervened.

This ritual of service is not yet extinct. Even in London there is still a remnant that adheres to it. I knew a Colonel who would "put in for leave" to conform with the Gaelic service in Crown Court. I went with him. The driver was inconceivably ignorant of our destination, although we explained to him our purpose. In despair we alighted in Covent Garden.

A grave man in black with two books in his hand, a woman by his side in more black still, and a small boy also in black, passed by. The boy walked as if his legs were broken. We knew that boy, and we followed — straight into the church.

To our astonishment, the minister who mounted the pulpit to preach the Gaelic was one with whom we had gone to School at Orwell. His name was Lamont, son of the elder of that name. He made no concessions; he did not even announce the name of the chapter in English. After the sermon was over, we heard some discussion of the minister's Gaelic. It appears there were Lewis people present, who pride themselves on the purity of their tongue, and they declared that this man must be a *Sgiathanach*. I made bold to ask a woman who was forward in the controversy wherein lay the distinction. She quoted a whole passage of the sermon as he uttered it, and then repeated it as it should be spoken. We could detect no difference. We were in the situation of the Lowlander who once confessed that he could observe no "dufference between dufference and dufference." In that place of worship I first discovered the natural use of the three-penny piece.

This psalmody did not meet every human need. Much of it seemed no longer pertinent to the life of the modern and western world. For the discontented there were, of course, the paraphrases; but their use was limited. The Reverend Gavin Lang, uncle of a future Archbishop of Canterbury, who was on the Island for a holiday, came to preach during an interregnum. From his name he seemed to be a safe man, and he was known to be Minister of St. Andrew's Church in Montreal, which was yet at that time in connexion with the Church of Scotland. In opening the service he announced a paraphrase to the crowded congregation. An elder — his name was James Mac-Kenzie — arose in his place, and with much gravity addressed the minister in the high pulpit. "Mr. Lang, we are not in the habit of using the paraphrases in the solemn worship of God's sanctuary." The minister accepted the rebuke in silence, and substituted the 100th psalm — All people that on earth do dwell — against which he supposed no possible objection could be alleged. But in the attempt to free himself from theological entanglement, he led the congregation into a liturgical difficulty, for the psalm he chose happens to be written in the eight-eight meter, and such lines cannot be declaimed. The Master, who was precentor for the day, cleverly substituted the second version of the same, which is written in the eight-six meter for that divinely preordained purpose.

Upon one occasion in the year two paraphrases were permitted, and they were sung without precentor. There were also five hymns that might be used on secular occasions; and one of these, which begins, "The hour of my departure's come," and ends, "Now let thy servant die in peace," was considered especially suitable in the hour and article of death. The Master was often called to assist at such events. They were considered too trivial to warrant the disturbance of the Minister at an untimely hour.

Of all the paraphrases the Master confessed that his favourite was :

> In life's gay morn, when sprightly youth
> With vital ardour glows,
> And shines in all the fairest charms
> Which beauty can disclose...
>
> For soon the shades of grief shall cloud
> The sunshine of thy days,
> And cares, and toils, in endless round,
> Encompass all thy ways.

As a summary of life this was not convincing. None of us had observed much gaiety in life's morn nor sprightliness in youth; and equally we hoped the miseries of advancing age were overstated.

Even this volume of traditional poetry proved to be inadequate. There was need for native expression. The religious emotion is at once the most diffuse and the easiest to express; its indulgence the most commendable or the least open to censure. The Minister so indulged himself in a printed book of hymns. As poetry it is not very good, but it has other excellencies. These hymns profess to relate the religious experience of the person who is fortunate enough to have "come through" the various processes of salvation from conviction to assurance; but the poet was compelled to restrain himself within the doctrinal limits prescribed by theological tradition.

If the poet were to become ecstatic in contemplation of the spirit, infinite, eternal, and unchangeable, in his being, wisdom, power, holiness, justice, goodness, and truth, he must recollect, lest others be led astray, that this same spirit has foreordained whatsoever comes to pass. He must remember too, that all mankind by their fall lost communion with that spirit, and by the sinfulness of that estate are under his wrath and curse, liable to all miseries in this life, to death itself, and to the pains of hell forever.

If he were to lose himself in the poetic idea of free grace and universal love, the fatal barrier would arise that only some were elected from all eternity to everlasting life. And this effectual calling with its consequent benefits was not to be demanded or achieved; one must be persuaded and enabled to accept the means of redemption. Even then, too high a degree of assurance must be checked by the remembrance that no mere man since the Fall is able in this life to live perfectly; he sins daily in thought, word, and deed. Upon such hard terms poetry must be a difficult art.

These hymns, notwithstanding their excellence, were to be kept in due subordination to more inspired utterances. They bore the imprint— To be used for practice only; but it was not specified to what end that practice led, whether to harmonious singing or to growth in other forms of grace. In effect, these hymns were sung "whilst the people were gathering." As the people lived far apart and came on foot through the woods, and as they governed their movements by the sun, the time of gathering was protracted. The hymns from their very length alone served admirably the purpose for which they were designed.

Some of them contained nearly two hundred lines. They were written in Gaelic or in English, and the most important were translated from one language into the other.

This poetry was classical in the sense that it expressed one at least of those powerful emotions that are perpetual and recurrent. It contained fresh observation, and was therefore modern, as Milton is modern, for he admits "artillery" into his heavenly battles; or Browning, who takes note of a window pane and "the quick scratch and the blue spirt of a lighted match." These two canons of Mr. Squire's criticism are completely illustrated in one passage from our hymnology : "Fall'n a prey to remorseless devils, we lay all trodden and peel'd." Dante has not done better. The first phrase is universal; the second is quite specific.

As the poet travelled the snow roads, he came upon "pitches," like the gulf between two billows. These were filled with young fir-trees cut from the forest. In the spring, when the snow disappeared, these young trees lay trodden in the mire, stripped of their bark by the incessant trampling of iron feet. As the young sinner looked upon these striplings, he might well say, "This is my body."

Many of the elders who had skill in the use of words and the pre-requisite religious experience tuned their lyres, as one of them has written, and their hymns in time were included in the semi-sacred book. In the summer of 1930, the daughter of this elder spent some days with us. She was slight and

beautiful as a wraith, and being eighty-six years old,
her voice was suitably thin for the pure melody. She
sang in Gaelic and English the hymns her father
had written nearly a hundred years ago; for he wrote
them the year he was "set free." Three years later,
she came again, but old age had done its work, as it
has done with even more famous singers. In this
choice of hymns the Master had great authority. The
authors would bring their verses, and he would fit
them with suitable tunes. They would then be circulated in manuscript form for general criticism.
Few survived the poetical and doctrinal tests.

There was in addition a body of secular poetry.
Much of it was printed on leaflets or in pamphlets,
and of this a large collection is preserved. It is in the
main descriptive, and only the most important events
are selected as themes : a riot, religious or political;
a shipwreck, a murder, an execution. Ten years after
the *Titanic* sank, a neighbour came in, and with
much excitement asked if we had heard of "the shipwreck." We confessed ignorance of any such disaster.
She said there was a woman in the kitchen, who had
the news in a poem from a cousin in Boston. The
woman was brought in, and she sang the complete
narrative of the tragedy of the ship "that lies full sixty
fathoms deep on the Banks of Newfoundland." From
this she continued her repertory and ended with the
account of a murderer who, "Sad to tell, this day has
fell, from where he stood, and got a check, with hem-
pen rope, around his neck."

After the American Civil War, the place was

invaded by soldiers' marching songs with a roaring chorus. Ten years later there was an invasion by evangelistic hymns which were about equal to the musical and religious capacity of a sophisticated negro. Before these the tender minor tunes and the simple poetry allied with them went down.

This once powerful church at Orwell has been rent by heresy and death, and is now sadly diminished in number. This diminution causes no concern. As an old elder observed, we have yet more followers than our Master had. In an address which the Reverend Father Hingston, rector of Loyola College, gave in a Unitarian church, he observed the evanescence of all religious institutions except his own, and in proof of his thesis pointed sadly to me as the last and sole survivor of the Church of Scotland on the mainland of America.

Only one minister remains, the last in America to keep intact connexion of any kind with the ancestral Church of Scotland. I have heard all the great speakers of the world; he is the only one I can endure with pleasure. If he speaks less than an hour one feels that one is defrauded. In that church have been witnessed all the heresies of ecclesiastical history. We did what we could, but there was no hand heavy enough to keep them down.

The last trial was only nine years ago. There were then three ministers, two of them brothers; the third fell into error over the doctrine of the resurrection, and he was cited before the presbytery of three. I asked one of the brothers if it would be commonly agreed that the heretic had had a fair trial.

"Yes," he answered me, "he will have his own vote." Before the day of trial the unfortunate man died.

"He has been called before a higher tribunal," I said to one of the brothers.

"Another tribunal," he corrected me.

The Church was concerned with itself alone; it never attempted to proselytise, or sent money to foreign missions, until eight years ago. There was a somewhat similar nucleus in Toronto, and help was given. To one who remonstrated with the Minister over this departure from tradition, he gave the assurance that they had the money, and thought "better to send it to Toronto than to the black heathen."

But an elder would always be sent where there was need. One year it was announced that Captain Grant would not be present at the sacrament. Fear was lest he might have considered that he had attained to so high a degree of perfection that this earthly communion was an act of supererogation — the heresy of pantheism. The fear was set at rest; he had gone to the Peace River, a journey of four thousand miles. His daughter was married there, and had been "under conviction" for six months. As it was not considered probable that she could obtain any help from the local ministers, her father thought best that he should go himself. She was "set free" the following winter.

To the older men theological speculation was a

continual mental exercise, and it took the form of spiritualizing the obvious meaning of scripture. Their only authority was the Bible; and when the Master died his loss was greatly deplored, as he was reputed to possess a book by which, if one gave him a single word, he could instantly find the text in which it appeared. There was now no man living "who could work that book." When I professed a familiarity with Cruden's *Concordance*, that was a proof that they were not forsaken. Philo and the early fathers, especially Origen, were masters in that form of exegesis, and their writings had long been an entertainment to me. I could give the "spiritual meaning" which should be assigned to every phrase, and in a short time found myself an authority which few would venture to dispute. Even the Master was astonished at this doctrine, and found in this skill a ready means to dispel the slander that one of his own had become a "free-thinker." On a famous occasion the stigma was fastened upon the most ruling elder by compelling him to admit, which he did with alacrity, that he thought upon all matters as "freely" as he could, and took his opinions from no living person.

This elder was greatly illuminated by the suggestion that the fourth Gospel was written by Lazarus. It solved his last remaining problem, and he spent a long winter in writing his *summa theologiae*. He made the discovery that it is easier to talk than to write; and when he had finished seven foolscap pages, he became so irritable that his conduct was intolerable to his family. His wife burned the manuscript, but she had exemplary punishment. As she returned from the sacrilege, she was stricken by a stroke, and suffered from paralysis for two years until she was released by death. The elder endured her sufferings as his own martyrdom, and as a warning that the world was not yet ripe for the revelation he proposed to make. Many similar writings are yet extant. When I am asked about publication, I always recommend the better way, that they be circulated in manuscript in accord with the admirable warrant of the earlier church, an advice which many secular authors might well take to themselves. Indeed that practice has been strongly urged in respect of the present writing by persons closely concerned in it.

When a man quotes as authority his own inner experience, it is impossible to controvert, convince, or contradict him. He is on the way to being a martyr. One day an unauthorized person — he was not even an elder — assumed "to lead the singing," and failed. The Minister asked him by what authority he did that thing. "By the authority," he declared, "of the Lord Jesus Christ, who saved my soul and set me free." The man was under the influence of strong religious emotion; his white collar had come adrift from the button at the back, and he seemed to suffer no inconvenience. The martyr's stake henceforth had less meaning for me. Confident in his own artistry, the Master took side with the Minister. He did not agree that music was automatically a benefit that either accompanies or flows from justification, adoption, and sanctification. He thought further, that in face of unrestrained freedom it was impossible to organize or maintain the church militant on earth. A similar discovery is now being made by more experienced persons.

It is probable in the western world at least that similar conditions will produce identical institutions. In that primitive church at Orwell a discipline was developed comparable in miniature with the practice of the European church in the time of Gregory. The members, especially when they had no sins to confess, confessed their sins one to the other and in public. Forgiveness was implored on their behalf, subject to their contribution and promise of amendment. In the interval they were placed under an interdict and denied the sacraments. As proof of their contrition, they accepted penance. A woman who erred was made to stand upright in face of the congregation whilst she confessed her fault, and absolution was implored for her. The Master himself endured the ordeal of discipline. He was degraded from the elders' bench, and compelled for three Sabbaths to sit with the laity. His sin was that in a hotly contested election he had voted for free public schools.

Therefore, to the Catholic practice of confession and penance the Master had no objection save that it was secret and easy. He was well aware that the priest joined his prayers with the prayers of the penitent one, imploring forgiveness; but he thought the private penance imposed as a sign of contrition was too slight. He was aware too that the priest did not grant absolution; at most he could only ask that the penitent be absolved from sin. In his own church the injunction, "confessing your sins one to another," was literally obeyed. That was the main subject of every conversation; but as the sins confessed were mainly doctrinal doubts, the confession passed into a boasting of the intellectual cleverness with which the doubts were resolved, and merely formed a premiss upon which an elaborate discourse was based. Nor did he object that the public service of the priest was in an unknown tongue. He thought it likely that the hearer of prayer understood Latin as well as English. His own children understood very little Gaelic, but he would not admit that ignorance as a bar to growth in grace.

Catholic families were not resented as such. On the contrary, they were treated with indulgence. Their religion was not their fault. It came as a wholesome surprise that they regarded their religion as the greatest blessing in their lives. Their children as a matter of routine studied the Shorter Catechism in the school; but they could not make much of it, although we gave them what assistance we could.

At home, it was recited aloud in unison, phrase by phrase, following the Master, who proclaimed the stops; comma, semi-colon, colon, period; and these were repeated as if they were an integral part of the divine revelation. It was at least an exercise in the punctuation of sentences. A younger child was more carefully instructed. To learn the relative value of these stops, he was compelled to recite : comma, one; semi-colon, one-two; colon, one-two-three; period, one-two-three-four.

Matters so simple, so well understood by us, and so lucidly explained, as the trinity, the sacraments, and the resurrection, remained for Catholic children "a mystery" until the end. Their parish priest was a wise man. He allowed they might at most learn to spell hard words and read long sentences; he would himself attend to all else. One thing, however, we could not understand, their tolerance of playing-cards. It was well known that Andy Gunnip had been accosted by the devil, as he returned from a party at which those emblems were used; and again, a persistent winner was accidentally discovered to have cloven feet. Late in life, the Master's wife herself took to the game, and against any remonstrance only urged, "Times have changed."

His teaching was that a person who attended sufficiently to his own religious affairs and the doctrine of his own church had neither time nor desire to concern himself with the practice or belief of persons born into a different faith; and he would cite by name the Morriseys, Macdonalds, Macleods, Mackinnons, families of upright, punctual, and religious lives, whose various beliefs seemed to be adequate for them.

But we did not consider ourselves protestants, since we protested against no one; still less presbyterians, since at the time we had no presbytery. When

Captain Grant was asked why it was that the pres-
byterian was the darkest of all religions, his answer
was prompt : "If the light is turned into darkness
how great shall that darkness be." Catholics we
considered as children striving towards the light. Our
doctrine of the Sacrament of the Lord's Supper was
identical with theirs. We did not consider it a
communal meal to which all might come. It was an
awful mystery in which the accidental fell away; the
material passed into the spiritual; and by a process
of thought the human was merged in the universal
divine.

This Sacrament was the event of the year. It lasted
from Thursday to Monday. People came fifty miles.
All work was suspended. Every house was filled, and
many visitors were billeted in barns. Thursday was
fast-day; Saturday for preparation; Monday for
thanksgiving. The church windows were removed,
so that those outside could hear the sermon and the
Master's splendid voice as he led the singing. The
tables were "fenced" and "tokens" taken up. An
elder was once seen to drag an unworthy person from
the table lest he eat and drink damnation to himself.
In early days the service would not be finished before
the sun had set. We still do what we can to keep alive
the spirit of the Sacrament. It brings us in contact
with old men of rich and beautiful nature. Ten years
ago we had for the occasion four guests, the youngest
of whom was seventy-six years old and the oldest
eighty-nine. As they turned to go, they each blessed
one another with a kiss, as the custom was amongst

old men in the Master's house.

One of the younger of these elders was a delicate humorist. He had been "set free" in the Master's house some seventy years before, and he would point to the precise spot at which that freedom was achieved, although it was really in the older house. He was son of a famous elder and poet, who "prayed so fervently that the sweat ran out of his shoes." On the Sabbath morning he offered "to sing a song," which he did from memory to the extent of seventy-two lines. The tune has since been made familiar by a famous comedian, and the words appeared to be wholly secular :

> O daughter, take good heed,
>   Incline, and give good ear;
> Thou must forget thy kindred all
>   And father's house most dear.

The jest was apparent only to the instructed. The song was "another version" of the 45th psalm.

After the Boer War, I was in Holland with my friend Karel Boissevain. His father had just come from seeing Paul Kruger who lay dying a few miles away. He was a serious man, and we talked of the reality of religion amongst simple people like ourselves and the Boers. When I told him of the importance to us of this annual event, he raised his hands in a splendid gesture of comprehension.

"I understand now," he cried, "what Kruger meant, when he declared to Chamberlain, that he could not attend to political matters at the time of the Sacrament."

It was well understood that, whilst every sin is deserving of wrath and curse both in this life and in the life to come, some transgressions are more heinous than others. To the Master the most heinous was Sabbath-breaking because it was the easiest to discover. To his wife the ultimate sin was untruthfulness, and cruelty. To the grandmother the chief commandment was, Honour thy father and thy mother, but that honour in the highest degree was due to herself by reason of her anterior parentage. Her exegesis might be correct, and the penalty was clear. The eye that despiseth to obey his grandmother the ravens of the valley shall pluck it out. The valley was there; the crows might be the ravens. A boy stricken in conscience would peer at the avenging birds from between his protecting fingers.

The Master continually reproached himself for his laxity in Sabbath observance. He could not vie with his neighbours who lived a less complex life. It is hard to be a saint in a cold climate; the drudgery of the body is so insistent. On the holy day the best people would not light a fire or draw water from the well. To cut wood was beyond question. There was the known case of the man who merely gathered sticks upon the Sabbath day, and the congregation stoned him with stones, and he died. One would not even shave himself on that day; he would as soon think of cutting wood. To cut wood was the ultimate act of defiance. Besides, the neighbours would hear the sound of the ax.

In every community there are conventions by which the status of the member is established, and the general safety preserved : Then said they unto him : Say now Shibboleth, and he could not frame to pronounce it right. Then they took him and slew him at the passages of Jordan. When Colonel Bowie, he of the bowie knife, made himself dictator of Texas, he proposed that any "Yankee" entering the territory should be hanged. The test was to be the word *cow*, exacted from every entrant at the frontier river. When the maritime isolation of Nova Scotia was threatened by the scheme to confederate the colonies into a Dominion, it was seriously proposed by a legislator who afterwards became Lieutenant-Governor that any person entering the colony by a land route should be hanged.

In England the population is clearly divided into two classes according to their treatment of the letter *h*. The upper class is again divided according to the time that elapses before a member reveals that he has been to Oxford or Cambridge. As a test of birth, breeding, and culture this rule is absolute. The most cultured Englishman I ever knew did not mention the matter once in thirty years, but it turned out that he had never been at any University. In Orwell the test of righteousness was the scrupulosity with which the Sabbath day was observed.

Yet there was another matter about which the Master's heart was troubled. This was the eating of forbidden food. The directions were quite clear, but for the most part inapplicable to any food likely to be found in that far place. The eagle, the ossifrage, the ospray, the vulture, the kite, the raven, the owl, the hawk, the cuckoo, the cormorant, the swan, the pelican, the gier eagle, the stork, the heron, the lap-wing, and the bat — about these there was no ques-tion. The camel too, and the coney, and the hare were immune because they did not exist. They might chew the cud and divide not the hoof, and therefore be unclean; but the injunction against the useful swine was equally specific. Though he divide the hoof, he chews not the cud; he is unclean. The Mas-ter's wife was content so long as the discussion re-mained abstract; but she made it clear that her dom-estic economy would be governed by experience; the family from which she came had always been notor-iously well supplied with pork, and suffered no harm.

A venerable elder came with great labour to him-self to remonstrate with the Master who had been in-veigled into the purchase of lightning rods for his house. Although the elder was upwards of ninety years old his zeal would not permit him to follow the road and enter by the gate. He must climb a fence and approach through a pasture in which was an amazing large sow with a miraculous litter of thirteen young and, worse still, completely black. These had become pets of the children and followed the stranger, loudly soliciting the favour of food. The Master heard the elder raging, and went to meet him at the foot of the garden in a conciliatory mood. He was exclaiming in passion, "I thought I had only come into the country of the Gadarenes, but now I behold Dagon on the top of your house." In the end he was mollified, and as he came to the door he was gracious enough to say to the Master, "I ever loved you, William."

By temperament the Master was easily moved to religious emotion. To his wife the expression of emotion of any kind appeared to be indecent. For excessive terms of friendship even, "sweetness" was her word, and she caricatured with bitter contempt persons so affected. Her objection to novels was of the same kind. They exposed secret things, and made them false by heightened colour. From the austere reticence of her early home she moved by marriage into an atmosphere of religious exuberance; but through sheer loyalty she never winced. On the Sabbath after her marriage she sat by her husband's side in church, once only; for after that ceremonial appearance men and women occupied different places. The text of the sermon read : Is there never a woman among the daughters of thy brethren or among all thy people ? She was embarrassed. She had come from Belle-Face.

She never winced; but equally she remained un-moved to the end. When she lay upon her death-bed, the religious enthusiasm of the Minister, himself since dead, was a sore trial to her. She spoke to the doctor. She had her own thoughts, she protested. The doctor was the son of a former minister who was austere and reticent as herself. With a long remem-brance of his own and her family life, the doctor

assured her, "You have heard enough preachin' —
and prayin' too," he added. As she repeated this
assurance, although it was in her last hours, she did
not forget to imitate his clipped words. This mimicry
was "so like the Smiths," as the Master would have
said.

She, so far as we were aware, never made any
open "profession of religion," although there was a
rumour that she had done so when her first child
was born. For women it was not considered necessary, proper or seemly. That practice was confined to
the Methodists. She once repeated the report that a
Methodist woman had prayed formally in the meeting, but she did not believe it. This reticence she
impressed, or transmitted unconsciously, upon all her
children. One of the torments of early life was the
continuous attempt, insidious or open, on the part
of the Master to violate that sense of personal right
to inner secrecy. Only one of his sons ever gave anything more than the most perfunctory consent to this
incessant demand.

One partial exception should possibly be made.
His eldest son, himself a doctor, at the age of thirty-
three came from the States to die. I made a journey
of a thousand miles to see him. He was suffering
from a painful and incurable malady for which mor-
phine was the only palliative. He spent the more lucid
intervals one long summer day in describing to me a
saloon he proposed to open in New York when he
was well. He displayed an exquisite taste in saloons,
especially upon the carved mahogany bar, the brass

rail, the chairs and tables, the decoration of the ceiling and walls. There were to be shining brass taps, ivory strikers, glasses of great size and delicacy. Upon the shelves would be oaken kegs of wine, brilliant bottles, and every bottle true to brand. He was very grateful to me for my visit, and in return promised to allow me to come behind the bar. Next morning he announced with sincere regret that he was not going to open the saloon after all, as he had made a profession of religion in the night.

"I am sorry to disappoint you," he said; "but you would not mind if you knew how pleased your father was to hear the excellent profession I made."

Death-beds rarely come up to expectation. The Master's eldest sister, Janet by name, is reputed to have died in darkness, but no one believed it. She was attended by her brother-in-law, a good but unlearned man. He was not a "praying man"; his ministration was confined to a reading of the scripture, and as he followed the practice of reading where the book opened, the choice imposed upon the sick woman was not always appropriate to her condition. His manner of reading caused her extreme irritation. He pronounced "spirit" as if it were spelled with an *e.*

At the funeral of the Master's wife, two additional ministers came as an act of courtesy. We consulted an experienced person as to the part that should be allotted to them. There was a certain risk. Her own minister never made use of the familiar chapter from Corinthians. It was a dangerous chapter he said, unless it were accompanied by proper exposition, and for that there was no time. The adviser decreed it might do no harm if one of them were allowed to read a piece in the Bible, "provided the chapter were set for him," and the other were to pronounce the benediction. As it turned out, instead of pronouncing the formal words of dismissal, he delivered a prayer which contained much debatable matter. These extempore prayers were frequently used as a delicate vehicle for conveying innuendoes or personal reproof. "Did you hear the dig I gave him in my prayer?" a minister once asked of her.

The Master's death was simple. We were sitting in the garden one Sunday afternoon in July. He seemed restless. I advised him to smoke a cigarette. He was doubtful. It was forty years since he had smoked, although he had used tobacco for fourteen years before that. He smoked half the cigarette and said, "This is not for me." In the evening he went to bed early. On Monday he did not arise; he was weak. On Tuesday morning he had some shortness of breath. At night he asked for his most favoured son to sit with him. There were two watches in the drawer to be wound. He explained the correct method of winding them. One other matter was heavy on his mind; there was a debt of forty cents owing to the blacksmith for removing the shoes from a horse: "One of yourselves will bring the money to him; and be careful not to ask for a receipt; the poor man does not write." Then he asked that the final chapter of Ecclesiastes be read to him. At the end of the seventh verse : Then shall the dust return to the earth as it was; and the spirit shall return unto God who gave it : he said, "I think that will do." His confessor called to me. When I came into the room the Master was already dead. Death comes when the emotions are exhausted.

XIV

THE WORLD OF NATURE

THAT new world was filled with the material of romance, with which a boy could fabricate a richer world of his own. From this necessity no child is exempt. Even the denizen of the town does his best, like a beaver in a menagerie striving to gratify an ancestral longing by building a dam with the mud and sticks at his command.

But at Orwell, any night a boy might hear the sound of guns, and feel a rush of wind; if he stood upon a hill, and the moon were full, he might even see the phantom ship of the dead pirates. Then he would know that some searchers were disturbing their treasure. It was well known that there were rich men who had gained their riches by finding hidden treasure; there was no other way; the efficacy of ten per cent was not understood.

"Old Myers" — this was a matter of common knowledge — had gone with two companions to dig for gold. When they were nearing the pot, they felt the wind; they heard the sound of guns at sea, but before they saw the spirit of the dead man who had been left to guard the treasure, two of them fled in fear. Their more hardy companion, they surmised, braved all the elemental forces, and secured the treasure; for he soon began to display signs of wealth, and had money to lend to anyone who asked for it with good security.

Witches, ghosts and fairies were so common they excited little interest. *Bocans* were a more serious menace. A *bocan* might leap upon a boy in the dark at any moment. Lights were seen; bridges would quiver in sign of an approaching funeral. There were interpreters of dreams and omens; and more inexplicable still, persons with the gift of second sight. By this power those who were about to die stood revealed; but there was a convention of honour that no name was to be disclosed until the event had occured.

A death-bed was a public spectacle to which a child was brought for edification, as a warning of his own latter end. I have yet before my eyes the spectacle of the blacksmith who, as I now know, was dying of pneumonia. There were two conventional signs that death had come into the community : the window of the sick room was seen to be open, or the chaff bed-tick was being burned in the garden.

A neighbour was working in the field. He looked fixedly across the valley. "Johnny Ban is dead," he announced.

"How do you know ? " I asked.

"The window of his bedroom is open." He was aware that the window was open to allow easy egress of the spirit from its earthly habitation. The advent of death must be announced at once to the whole family connexion. To neglect any member was a sign of ostracism, and the message must be received before the victim was "on the boards."

But there was also the living world of growth. The Master's wife had a love for every growing thing, especially for flowers. In the winter, she kept potted plants, and her final task at night was to remove them, as many as three dozen, to the cellar, where they would remain safe until the house was warm on the following day. From every journey she would bring home a slip, a flower, or a shrub. She planted them in any obscure place known only to herself, and a child had to move with care lest he did damage. Occasionally they grew, and a child would be set to weed away the thicket of grass that surrounded them. Once it was a bed of dahlias that showed through the grass. He conceived the plan of removing the flowers gently, and then with heavy strokes to dig the ground, rake off the roots, make all smooth, and then replant the precious flowers. But she came upon the scene before the design was complete, and saw only the devastated area.

Her solicitude for a plant was so great she would not allow it to be pruned. Roses ran wild; shrubs sent up suckers that grew into ungainly trees. When in time the garden became a jungle, the utmost she would permit was that a branch be tied back with a piece of string; it must not be allowed to feel the pain of iron. The flowering trees she loved best of all; and of these the chief were the acacia, the locust, and the lime, admirable when kept under control, a nuisance when allowed to overrun the place.

But to all objectors she had her answer on a summer day when she looked up into the sky and beheld the heavens filled with flowers, and heard the bees murmuring like surf on a distant shore. If on that day the humming-bird came to the honeysuckle she kept for this convenience, her triumph was complete. Upon one scene of beauty she would not look. She would not look upon the earth in time of silver thaw. The new-fallen snow tinged with pink and violet, the crystal trees sparkling and flashing in the strengthened sun — to look upon that was not just to the spectacle which had been prepared, eternal in the heavens. She chose to wait until her appointed time.

It was only after her death that we ventured upon an attempt to recreate a garden from what had become a wilderness. A heavy north-east gale had searched out every native aged tree and every exotic feeble-rooted one. One of these was a balm-of-Gilead, a large tree before we acquired the place, the tree from whose top we first surveyed the larger world, which indeed was a landmark for a child who went abroad. When I heard it was fallen, I looked to see it lie as long as the giant's bean-stalk up which Jack climbed. In reality it was itself nothing more than a sprawling giant. As we burned the wood in the fireplace, the grandmother had her revenge. She hated that tree for the cotton-like refuse it shed once a year. The destruction of that tree was a subject of annual discussion between the two women. Now, discussion is at an end; all three are gone.

For a vine she had a gentle hand. A tendril wandering in the wind was like an orphan wanting support. She had the buildings covered with vines, so that the repair of any fabric must be done subject to their need. But the vine and flower she loved best of all was the trailing arbutus, the Mayflower of the Canadian spring. Her first excursion after the winter was gone, and snow lay only in shady places, was to the moist woods in search of those small pink flowers on their glistening vines. For these excursions her strength did not fail until the very end. Sure-footed and agile as a girl, she would traverse the stream on a fallen log if there were plant or animal on the yonder side that excited her curiosity.

This adventure was not so simple a matter as it might appear. The conventions of that life were strict, and the place was so thickly settled that any person who moved abroad was under a wide surveillance. Any such movement was a matter of comment, surmise, and speculation. A grown woman wandering towards the woods might well be suspected of being "queer." There was a deeper reason for caution, as it was well known that women going to the woods in search of cattle, for example, might be waylaid, possibly with their own consent or even by their own design. It had been reported that an astute fellow was in the habit of providing himself with a cow-bell by which he lured innocent women into the forest. A young man in that place who wears strange clothes, lets his hair grow long, or walks with his hat off is still in danger, even if he is a professor, of being put in the asylum.

When the Master's wife went upon the annual adventure of searching for spring flowers, she stilled all tongues by letting it be supposed that she was going for sand. She carried with her a small tin dish and a strong spoon. In the fall of the year enough white sand was laid in for keeping the kitchen floor white during the winter, and the excellence of a woman's housekeeping was judged by the whiteness of her floor. The use of sand saved soap, and that was important where the making of soap was part of the economy of the house.

XV

THE OPEN DOOR

THE Master's wife in time found herself with ten children for whom she felt a certain responsibility that they be established in life. The Master also felt himself responsible, but he was concerned entirely with the life to come. He considered his whole duty done if their souls were saved, even by the skin of their teeth. His task was the harder of the two. It included the lesser, for he had made the important discovery, that if the kingdom of heaven were assured, all things else would be included in that. To this end he kept in continuous operation the plan of salvation, as set forth by various authorities under his hand, and by his own inner experience.

But his wife was more impressed by the virtue inherent in "early training." Lady Grey, with her rare intelligence and tact in directing the conversation to a subject of which the person addressed might be supposed to know something, once asked her at what age one should begin the training of a child, and tentatively suggested seven years. In instant alarm the mother assured her that a child might be already ruined at seven days. The grandmother likewise had her remedy against an unruly infant, which was "to put it above the clothes." A moment's exposure to the winter air, she had found, would persuade any child to accept warmth and quiet in contentment.

The worldly outlook before these ten children was not promising; yet the parents faced their future with unconcern. They relied upon the experience of the psalmist which was even more profound than their own; "I have been young," he said, "and now am old; yet have I not seen the righteous forsaken, nor his seed begging bread." The father was careful to explain that this was "spiritual bread"; the mother held that we stood to gain both ways.

She had made the further observation that the school was the open door of escape for those who could enter it. Upon that her mind was fixed. The law was absolute. Every child was sent to school every day in the year, except during the three weeks of vacation in the spring and in the fall, intervals arranged, not because they were the most suitable for the enjoyment of holidays, but because the scholars were required at home for the work incident to those seasons. No matter how pressing the work, it was to be done before and after hours; if that time did not suffice, the boy could run home at the noon recess, and complete. The school saw to it that home lessons were not neglected.

The Master's wife had no illusions. Learning was for advancement only. She had heard her uncle say that mathematics was coming into use as an aid to navigation in foreign seas. True, he himself had never felt the need, but he only sailed the North Atlantic, which was nothing more than a ferry. He followed the line of fifty as if it were a blazed path through the woods; and if he were blown off to the north or south, he worked his way back to the line by the help of his cross-staff, and shaped his course anew. He considered it providential that this line of fifty cleared the south coast of Ireland; those who sailed the great circle courted disaster. Longitude did not matter; he carried on all sail, and could not go any faster by knowing how much of his course he had run. Eyes and lead could tell him when land was near. His mate had a book of tables; but there was grave danger of running the finger down the wrong column; and a ship was too precious to be entrusted to the right reading of a set of figures. And yet, she was convinced that for sailing the great circle of the world, learning was the thing.

It was no part of any master's business to teach; his business was "to hear the lessons," in proof that they had been learned. If they were not learned, the boy was whipped; if he had to be whipped repeatedly, that was proof that he could not learn, and had better devote himself to some more useful occupation. None of her children suffered for unlearned lessons except from a neurotic and brutal peasant, "a marvellous severe and cruel schoolmaster," as Cranmer's also was. The remembrance endures : he too must now be a very old man if he is yet alive. The class was of ten boys, the word "separate." Beginning at the foot each boy spelled the word correctly, and each boy was promptly whipped. The boy at the head, when his turn came, spelled the word correctly, but with an air of defiance. The master had a moment of irresolution; he looked on his book, and found he was wrong. His handsome comment to his victims was, "If you did not deserve it this time, it will make up for the times you deserved it, and did not get it." But every examiner has his own test of scholarship.

In the army it was one of my duties to examine the educational attainments of boys who desired a commission. That word "separate" was the test-word. One boy spelled the word "sepperete." I had an instinct that he must have some vast compensatory qualification. Shakespeare wrote *scilens* : "the rest is silence." I passed him for the flying corps, which did not demand very high attainment in letters. The boy justified me in his career, and in his death.

Sir Archibald Macdonell, general officer commanding the 1st Canadian Division, had a method that was equally simple in selected cases. When a man appeared before him with a Highland name, he would ask him to repeat the battle-cry of his Clan. If he could utter it in Gaelic, he was recommended for a still higher grade. Colonel Cyrus Peck, V.C., was another who had achieved a similar simplicity. His method was to ascertain if a candidate for a commission could spell General Macdonell's name correctly. The test was not so trivial as it seems, for there are five possible ways in which the name may be spelled, and to misspell a Highland name is proof of an ignorant mind. Colonel Peck, in addition to being a wearer of the Victoria Cross was a member of parliament. It was my privilege to return from overseas in his company, and he affirmed that, the war now being finished, it was his intention to have a law passed, "compelling all these Macs to spell their name in the same way." He did not care how they spelled it; "let them agree among themselves." When he merely uttered General Macdonell's name, he unconsciously consulted a slip of paper which he drew from his pocket. He had struggled too long with those Highland eccentricities.

The masters in that Orwell school felt that their whole business was done when they kept order, so that those who desired to learn were left free in silence. This system of education had much to recommend it. No boy was compelled to attend school; he was not inveigled into a scholastic course which he was too feeble-minded to pursue; he was not beguiled from the land to fall into the abyss that lies on the hither side of a profession. Best of all, he was returned to the land or to a trade before he was rendered incapable of dealing with them. The school was always overcrowded. Every boy driven out enriched the land, and saved the expense of enlarging the school or hiring another teacher.

The school was not a prison. If a boy felt that he had no mind for words and abstract ideas, he was free to save and strengthen such mind as he had by exercising it upon events and things. There was also a fair degree of certainty in going to the land, or a trade, or the sea, that he would pass a useful and happy life, and die in his own bed rather than in the public ward of an alien hospital. Many of the boys who "ran away to sea" would come back in a year or two as serious young men, with pea-jackets of pilot cloth, peaked caps, large silver watches secured by a golden guard with cross-barred links like an anchor-chain. After some further years before the mast they discovered that entrance into the class of mates and master was denied to them from lack of education. They would come for a winter to study navigation; and before they were twenty-two years old they would return again, sailing into a home port as master of a square-rigged ship with a parrot in the cabin, a negro or Chinaman in the galley, and a monkey at the cross-trees.

These young men gave to the school a sense of reality, and helped the master to preserve discipline. In the grandfather's school was a well grown lad who was there for no serious purpose, and was a disturbance to pupils who desired to learn. The master, addressing one of those sailors said :

"Mr. Roche, you are a sailor ? "

"Yes, sir."

"Accustomed to obey orders ? "

"Yes, sir."

"Then level me that man." Mr. Roche with a single blow brought the offender to the floor, and then dragged him out of the school.

The properties of a school-master were few but conventional. They comprised a silver watch, a bifurcated leather strap, and a sharp knife known as a pen-knife. The strap was the emblem of his office; skill with the knife was a proof of scholarship. Boys brought their own quills; he fashioned the pen. With one long stroke he brought the goose-quill to a point, then snipped off the end, and with an incision against his thumb-nail split the nib. The steel pen was resented by parents on the ground of expense, and by the master as a contempt of his art. As a rule, in the earlier days he had no settled home, but lived with each family for a week in turn. His presence during that week was held to be of disciplinary value to the children, and also to himself, for it served to establish his written reputation for "sobriety."

The farm at Orwell provided the main body of food for thirteen persons at no other cost than the labour of procuring it. The Master's salary as Inspector of Schools ensured that his family lived in decency and comfort. But the work was done by children with the help of a man hired for labour beyond their physical strength. At such times the Master also worked, but his hands were soft; and although he worked with great vigour for the moment, he would soon remember some important duty like the writing of a letter. He gave the impression, however, that he could continue indefinitely at the same speed, if only he were free to give all his time to the work.

Every hour had the duty foreordained for it; there was little time for sportive exercises, none for boredom. To skate on the ice, to slide on the snow, to swim in the sea, meant work left undone or lessons unlearned. Work itself was converted into a game, with this distinction, that a game could be stopped when the interest flagged; work had set bounds; it must be finished. To finish a lesson or a piece of work was a pleasure even greater than the winning or losing of a game. No child suffered from the intolerable burden of continuous play, nor were parents bewildered in the effort to provide entertainment that never ceased.

Each child worked beyond his strength because there was a younger aspirant for every task as soon as it had become easy; and though strength and skill increased, work was always done in distress. There was no far-seeing and continuous control. Things were hardly done because they were done too late. On a farm the delay of a moment at a critical time will disorganize the operations for a year. Late sowing means late and damaged grain; late planting means work in autumn wet and cold. Soil hastily prepared grows weeds or nothing. With neighbours it was different. Farming was their sole occupation. Everything was ready in advance for seed-time, harvest, and winter.

With us, farming was subsidiary to all else. There were irruptions of visitors who must be cared for; ministers came, and stayed, with their families; aunts arrived at inopportune times; and all must be driven to and from boats and trains at all hours of the day and night over broken roads and breaking ice. Permeating the whole fabric was the mother's resolve to make a good appearance; and by catering to strangers she was compelled to neglect her own. By sheer force of will she subdued all to her own mood; affection for her was motive enough for striving to the uttermost to aid her in her distress. But the labour was joyless because it was so vaguely spent. We worked thinking only of escape.

Not one of us remembers the time when his mind was not dominated by this desire. But there was no escape. The blacksmith's forge looked hopeful, but he was a grimy man. The carpenter was poor, and he had a brood of ill-kept children. The boy in the country store was a dirty fellow, and clerks from the town had impudence and smartness beyond our reach. Far on the horizon was the doctor, but he seemed to live at the end of another existence. There was the ministerial calling, but that demanded an inner change of which we had little hope; and lawyers had a bad name.

When a child arrived at the age of three years he was of some service. He could fetch a stool, a broom, or a dish. At four he could hold a stick in his hand, and like his most primitive ancestor was then master of the animal creation, the cat, the dog, the hen, the goose, the sheep, the pig; and a little later on as his courage increased he could control the cow and even the horse. The Master's wife, when a girl, came upon a bear in the woods, eating a sheep. She picked up a stick for her protection, and felt quite safe, but did not attack the bear "as the sheep was already dead."

When a child was five he could go upon an errand. In the winter, by reason of his lightness he could run upon the crusted snow without sinking; in summer, when it rained, he could run between the showers by reason of his fleetness of foot. That was the fiction, and if he did sink in the snow or become wet in the rain, no harm was done. A child was an asset, not a liability or a problem, as he is in circum-stances where he must be supported until he is twenty years old, and depends upon his father to buy a razor for him to shave the whiskers off his face.

These errands gave entrance into the world. The earliest errand was going to the post-office, a distance of one mile, three times a week. The road lay up a slope, and along the level where the sea was visible, down a steep hill, and across tide water by an immense bridge. Many things could be seen — a flock of plover or other wild birds, a musk-rat in the marsh, or a fishing-boat on its way to the sea.

The post-office was kept by an Irishman named Barny; it was not known that "Barny" was the same as Bernard. He was a kind man, and always had a whimsical word. He was a tailor by trade, and carried on all his business sitting cross-legged on his table. He was short and stout, and conveyed the impression that he never walked. It was not the custom to keep postage stamps in the house. Money was carried, and the official affixed the stamps as if he were a notary. Barny had a heavy face with loose moist mouth which was kept still more moist by the continual use of a clay pipe, and he removed the surplus moisture with the cloth on which he worked. He was admirably equipped for affixing postage stamps, and it was presumed that he had been appointed for that physical reason. To go to the post-office was going into a new world, made still more strange by the swarthy children to be seen in his house. When he died, the Master's wife made a formal visit of condolence to the widow, and brought home a moving account of her sorrow and loneliness, which was the greater "as her man had always been with her in the house."

All business was transacted by messenger; the post would do very well for carrying a letter to Australia. I was ten years old before I saw a telegraph line, and fifteen when I saw a railway train. When the return journey amounted to fifteen miles, or when great speed was demanded for lesser journeys, a boy was allowed the use of a horse, at first bare-backed, and after he had acquired sufficient skill, with a saddle. The short legs were thrust into the leathers; and when the stirrups could be reached, that was a sign of maturity. In summer, travel was by wagon; in winter by sleigh. Between the seasons the situation was difficult.

The river Hillsborough lay between Orwell and the town. In summer it was crossed by a steam-ferry; in winter on the ice. The place of crossing was half a mile wide; the tide ran strong. When the boy reached the river in spring or fall, and the ferryboat was not running, he was faced with a serious problem. He must first decide if he would venture his horse or proceed on foot. He might skip across the floating masses of ice, leaving the horse behind; or he might proceed several miles up-stream where the ice was firmer, and crossing on foot test the ice with a pointed

stake. Depending upon the decision, he would return
for his horse, and putting him to a gallop might cross
in safety the heaving and crashing ice.

The horse might go through, but again the water
might be shallow, depending on the tide. The boy
might lose his horse, but such a calamity was so
extreme it was not to be thought of. It was like the
contingency of hell, so dreadful there must be some
escape from it. If he came to open water, flowing
black and deep, he could continue up stream until he
came to the end of the crack. To return home on the
mere pretext that the river was impassable — that
was a confession of failure too ignominious. Better
to lose his horse and himself too. Death explains
itself; failure does not. A boy so trained finds nothing
hard in life — or in war either.

Of one thing we were all convinced from the first:
we would escape from the land and the ice. We were
entirely of the opinion of the first man Adam, when
he found himself condemned to make his living out
of the soil. From our own experience, short as it
was, we came to his conclusion : that the ground was
cursed, that those who eat of it eat in sorrow, that
thorns and thistles are its natural product, and that
it was only by the sweat of one's face that one could
live by the land at all. Of the truth of this record I
was certain, but I doubted the sequence of events. I
made the discovery for myself, that it was his present
misery that compelled our first parent to invent an
anterior sin as the possible cause of a fate so
intolerable. At any rate, we had committed no sin,

and would not submit.

The common method of escape was "to run away to sea." There were ships in every port. Boys from the school had taken that desperate road; but too many came back, wearing top-boots, heavy trousers, woollen shirt, and a knife in the belt. Besides, their flight was taken in anger; they had been beaten. The boy would then go to the barn, gather a dozen eggs, sell them at the shop for ten cents, and with that as an equipment made his way to the nearest port. A boy who had proceeded more regularly was reputed to have done well. Next year I saw him on board ship, looking handsome in a uniform of some kind; but I observed that one of his duties was to take the Captain's cap, and I suspected he was in the wrong way.

For older persons the method was "to go to Boston," and many returned with an air of prosperity. But it was reported by one who went there "on a trip," that he had seen a boy in charge of a pair of horses, whose business it was to hook on to a tram-car, and help it up the hill. The spectacle seemed to belie the glowing accounts of ease and dignity that were prevalent. The truth is, our case was hopeless by reason of the affection we had for father, mother, and for the younger children; hopeless because this emotion seemed to be identical with weakness and cowardice. The fear in each heart was that he might be forced to accept one of two alternatives, either to work with his hands or to become "an agent," although we had not the slightest idea how such a person made a living. But there were forces at work, immediate as well as ancestral, of which we knew nothing. The immediate force was the resolve of the Master's wife that every child should learn his lessons. When I was eight years old, I acquired a Latin grammar. There were no definite classes in the school, and a boy was free to present himself in any subject he chose, subject to the usual penalty. I could make nothing of the book. It was quite clear that *mensa* meant table. How *of a table* was to be translated passed comprehension. There appeared to be no Latin for *of* or *a*. I consulted a mature scholar. He received me with derision and a suggestion of dis-honesty on my part. It was considered as infamous to help a boy in his lessons as to assist him secretly at an examination. But the vocabulary at the end of the book could be learned. The declensions could be examined as a mechanism. Suddenly the whole nature of the Latin cases burst upon me. I was set free from work forever. The life problem was solved. I was upon some peak from which I surveyed all the kingdoms of this world, and knew that they were mine.

At this time there was a new master. The first business of the boys was to try his temper, as a company of sappers would "feel out" a new major. One of the boys, a younger brother, went too far. He was summoned to the desk, and bade hold out his hand. The master with a chuckle of laughter gave him a playful tap with a penholder. The boys were beaten at their own game. A new era had dawned.

Fighting, swimming in the mill-ponds, playing ball were no longer capital offences. They were rather encouraged, and therefore lost much in interest. Instead, in that generous atmosphere, there was an outburst of scholarship.

Parents were told in private that their boys were wasting their time. Others were encouraged to give their more promising boys a better chance. It was at this moment I came forward with my new-found Latin. At the age of twelve I was reading Caesar, at thirteen the Greek testament. I had already mastered four books of Euclid, much algebra, the mechanical parts of French. Subjects taught in English were far in the past. The teacher himself was a scholar. He too was striving for college and university, for bursaries and scholarships. To be adopted into that number was a precious privilege reserved only for the elect. From that school, which never had more than two rooms, have issued 153 scholars who afterwards proceeded to university degrees.

XVI

THE ESCAPE

THERE was a scholarship in which anyone might aspire. I fixed my mind upon it, as if it were a piece of secret prey, but made no announcement of the intention. That might appear to be a boast or presumption, or even an act of folly that must be stopped. When the time came I was compelled to disclose the secret, as formal request for examination had to be made through the Inspector of schools, who was the Master. He received it without enthusiasm, and agreed as a concession. I felt free to point out to him, however, that the work of preparation had not involved any neglect of ordinary duties. The subjects were Greek, Latin, mathematics, French, English, and history; and the contents of all the textbooks were neatly bestowed in one little head.

For this first adventure into the world I was well dressed. From the eldest brother I had inherited a jacket of fine black Italian cloth. He had bought the material out of a foreign ship, and had it made by a sound tailor, but he never liked it. The sleeves were too long for me. The Master was content that they be turned back in form of a cuff, or at most cut off with the scissors; but the mother, saying nothing, removed the sleeves and shortened them from the shoulder. She had in the house a pair of linen cuffs embroidered at the edge. With these for a bosom she fashioned a white shirt. I have had nothing since from Bond Street that was finer or more fashionable.

The examination was to begin on the afternoon of a Wednesday, and it was my secret design that I should proceed to the town by a steamer that sailed the evening before from the Brush wharf, some three miles away. But the mother announced that she would herself drive me to the town in the morning. I surmised a fear in her heart lest I might fall into "bad company" during the night. Up to that time I had never slept a night away from home, and towns were well known to be dangerous places. This fear is in the heart of every mother. Professor Mavor tells me that he was once in Iceland, some thirty miles from the capital, in a house where a situation precisely similar had arisen. The mother would have her son stay at home, as she had heard that "Reykjavik was a very wicked city."

We had not gone a mile in the morning when we encountered a man coming from the southward alone in his wagon on the way to town. She recognized him as "Old Roberson," and asked him if he would take "this little boy" to town. She used the diminutive to suggest the lightness of the burden he was asked to assume. He agreed, I thought, without enthusiasm. The transfer was made and she turned homewards. I was afraid of him. I had heard of his oppression. He was small, dark, shaven, with black shining eyes.

The men I knew and trusted were tall, fair, bearded and blue eyed. My plan of operation was quickly formed. I could of course leap from the wagon at the first sign of violence; but I could not walk the eighteen miles in time for the examination. Instead, I resolved to strangle him, if he attacked me, throw his body from the wagon, and drive on alone to my fate.

He soon showed a keen interest in every farm we passed. I suspected he had a universal mortgage upon them, and was appraising their value. He would turn his head and begin to count all the objects he saw. Presently he evoked my assistance, and set me counting geese, sheep, cattle, plover. He praised me for my alertness and accuracy, and would then descant upon the nature of the objects we saw. It was many years before I discovered that this mysterious man was mysterious only because he was a sardonic humorist.

Three miles from the town he pretended that he had a call to make, and I must walk the rest of the way. I could run that short distance. When he saw my alacrity, he observed wheel tracks upon the man's place, and allowed he must have gone to town where they could meet. At the ferry he took me by the hand and wished. me good luck. I gave him a peppermint lozenge, which he put in his mouth with much gravity, and thanked me.

This scholarship was rather a formidable affair. There were only two of them for Queen's County; and they were open for competition to all the pupils in 180 schools, that is, to over 5000 persons. The actual number of candidates was 150; the chance of success was not large. The examination lasted two days. On the third all assembled to hear the result. The teacher, John Mackinnon, was on the platform. The list was passed to him. His handsome face broke into a heavenly smile. A secret emotion came upon me. It has been repeated seven times : once when disaster was converted into triumph by a left-hand mashie stroke at the Pit-hole in North Berwick; again in the Royal College of Surgeons; yet again at daybreak in a troop-train when I learned that the King had conferred the honour of knighthood upon me — and on four other occasions. When I returned home, the mother said nothing; the Master made some observations that seemed irrelevant; the grand-mother said, "Well, what else would you expect ? " She remembered, part in sorrow, part in pride "that none of your father's name ever worked." The long tradition of scholarship was unbroken.

In the autumn of that year I entered the Prince of Wales College with the scholarship, which was sufficient to pay fees and expenses. The principal was Alexander Anderson. Of the many teachers I have since known he was the best. His authority was absolute; therefore he was never known to exercise it. He was of short and massive frame, erect and unbending. He had a powerful head, beautifully modelled, with brilliant dark and humorous eyes, abundant grizzled hair that stood up as straight as himself, and a well cut beard. His dress and linen were faultless; his deportment as if he were a sergeant-major on parade; his grey beaver hat and golden stick were symbols of majesty.

He had two hundred scholars under his control, and in two years he never administered to any one so much as a rebuke, unless a whimsical bantering reference to youthful folly might be construed as such. He treated the crude boys as if they were grave young gentlemen determined to become scholars and win by their scholarship any highest place in the world. But he was known to have an immense reserve of savage sarcasm which none but a fool would let loose. A breach of discipline was looked upon by himself and his pupils as an offence against his own dignity and therefore against the eternal order of the universe. He had for his support the whole official community. Members of the government, of the judiciary, and of the professions had all passed through his school, and they retained for him a respect and fear not unmixed with affection. In addition the best schools were taught by his pupils, and they helped to propagate the legend of his power. Even the Master who was Inspector of those schools came under the spell.

He loved to teach. That was his secret. The subjects were few — Greek, Latin, mathematics, English, French. The only concession he made to the modern spirit was one hour a year in natural philosophy, but it was spent in the spirit of jest. His appliances were a large magnet, a Leyden jar, an enormous stick of red sealing wax, a wet battery, and an air pump. He never deigned to manipulate this machinery, but would stand by with an air of sardonic amusement, whilst his son delivered a current of electricity into a semi-circle of the newer boys with joined hands, or exploded a square bottle by extracting the air.

For English, Shakespeare was his text. He would read whole plays and expound their setting. That was his method of teaching ancient history. He would devote a day in turn to the masters of English prose, reading from their writings and describing the circumstances in which they were written. That was his method of teaching modern history. There were text-books, of course, of Greek, Roman, and English history, and of English literature; but these texts were learned in seclusion, and by "learning" was meant the ability to repeat them word by word as one would say the ten commandments.

This teacher had the curious idea that boys came to school to learn; not to waste their time, or their parents' money; and certainly not to play games. If they required work or exercise, the farm was the better place. It was well understood that the intention in coming to school was to escape from work by sitting in a professor's chair or on a judge's bench, by standing in the pulpit or before the altar, or moving at leisure in professional or political office.

Latin and mathematics were the media alone in which the boy's mind could be forged and tempered into a sharp, hard, and flexible weapon. There was no deception. He must learn them if he could. The text was before him. Translations were infamous; notes a subject of derision; the dictionary was enough. Virgil could be learned like a psalm; Horace like the lyrics of Burns; and Cicero like the speech of any other politician.

Greek as a discipline was not highly thought of. It was too interesting, too vivid and vital, not much better than French. It was taught by an old Irish gentleman called Gaven who had learned his classics in Rome. They were to him as his native tongue, and he read the Greek with a continuous chuckle over its ease and beauty. His theory was that anyone could learn Greek who listened with attention to his reading. In his hands, moods, voices, and declensions were merely devices for a precise and delicate expression of the ideas that arose in precise and delicate minds.

In that school there were few rewards. The choicest was the privilege of coming at eight in the morning, instead of nine, to a special class for Greek composition, conducted by Anderson himself, whereby the pleasant levity of his colleague was effectually met. There was only one other teacher, Thomas Lepage. He was not yet twenty years old. He died soon. He was a poet. From him a boy could learn by way of Wordsworth that there was an inner and intimate world of poetry. He was a man of the spirit. He dared to test his own skill upon the sonnet form.

The remembrance of one remains :

Westward I chanced to look, ere yet
    the night
Fell on a day of clouds, to note
    what sign,
If any, on the horizon might out-
    shine
Of a fair morrow, and there met
    my sight
Astonished a long line of silver
    light —
Off in whose soundless ae'ry depths
    divine
Peeped the faint stars, and drew
    these eyes of mine
Far hence, as native to some orb
    more bright.
So sometimes come to the tired
    spirit of man
Glimpses of rest and home; and
    for a space
He feels the breath of Heaven upon
    his face.
Glad earnest of the glory yet to
    be,
When light and Love shall
    compass earth's round span
Even as the waters fill the hollow
    sea.

At the end of two years in the Prince of Wales College I gained the usual certificate. For three months I taught in a school where the Master and his father before him had been master. At Christmas I secured the coveted Fanning Grammar School, and at the age of eighteen I was drawing a salary of three hundred and eighty dollars a year. No earthly power could touch me. I was free of work forever.

Malpeque, seat of this *studium generale,* the Master would have considered a worldly place. It was the oldest settlement on the Island, rich, compact, and completely civilized. There was a handsome church, an educated minister, two services a day. If he had suggested that his congregation were "sinners," they would have received the news with polite amusement. An evangelist was regarded as a curiosity, as a diversion. One of these was much encouraged by the large attendance. He asked those who were "saved" to stand up. No one moved. Moderating his appeal, he asked those who "desired to be saved" to stand up. The result was no better. Then, with a touch of irony, he appealed to all who wished to lead a "better life." The only response was from a low fellow who was known to be a fool and was suspected of being a thief. "Happy people," the evangelist exclaimed, and abandoned that cultivated field.

They were happy people, shrewd, kind, fond of gaiety and jest; and the old took their pleasures with the young. In appearance also this was a new world. As one came over the hill the place lay in a series of headlands, and gentle fields projected into the outermost ocean. For nearly three years I frequented those cliffs and waves, and heard the continuous sound of the sea. On a summer afternoon I would row my boat so far that the land was lost in the distance and the dark, meditating upon strange things.

For the first time I learned, what I always suspected, that humanity is not one, but a congeries

of families each with a unity of tradition, a similarity
of interest, an equality of education, an identity of
thought, manners, and morals; a "society" in which
the upper members could of their own free will
penetrate to the bottom; in which the lower members
could only by sheer merit and incredible difficulty
rise to the top. In that small place were descendants
of governors, judges, ministers, and statesmen; land-
owners, physicians, merchants, all with a pride in
their own class, and all living in harmony.

But the tragedy of the well born immigrant is the
inevitable destruction of his family; the reward of the
ill born may be the elevation of his. The resultant
level is democracy, the mass possibly raised, the
unusual destroyed. Those immigrants into Canaan,
of whom we have the most passionate account, faced
the peril of marrying with the children of the earth
by exterminating the original possessors of the land,
and resisting with equal courage any subsequent
invasion.

Those Highland communities did their best to
preserve the purity of the stock. A new arrival was
fenced about with prejudice, rumour, and convention,
lest his children might corrupt the community in
manners, morals, or religion. It was only after rigid
scrutiny he was adopted into the number, but for
thirty years he would be described as "an imported
man." One Englishman brought with him an
Esquimau wife, and henceforth all English were
regarded with grave suspicion. This woman would
fashion a pair of mitts or a waistcoat for a boy from

the skin of a grey seal he had caught in the bay. But after two generations of solitude the family disappeared to the States.

More instructive still, there was in Malpeque a segregated class which provided labour for the more menial tasks. They were admitted to the houses only on sufferance : they ate by themselves; they were treated with good-humoured toleration, their manners and morals a source of amusement. Twice a year I spent three weeks at Orwell. The Master was quick to notice a change, and between him and his wife there was veiled reference to the distinction between proper pride and false pride. When I left that school, the younger children wept. They had called me Master.

On the way into the mysterious world to a great University, oppressed by a sense of inexperience and ignorance, I was striving even at that desperate moment to repair this unworthiness by reading Greek prose composition. A senior student also on his way discovered me at the task. "Put that book away," he said, "and tell them you come from the Prince of Wales College." I told them so, and they admitted me to the second year, where I found myself in a class of grown men who were reading the journalistic Xenophon as if he were a serious author. From this I sought refuge in the library. It was the university library that destroyed me. In Malpeque, I had access to Dr. Kier's library, which he had inherited from his father, and enriched with his own books. His father was a minister and a scholar, and his house was a seminary where young ministers had been educated. The library was rich in the Fathers, in theology, and philosophy; but there was nothing much more modern than Matthew Henry's *Exposition of the Old and New Testament,* of the year 1708. I read them all, but it required three years. When I went to the university the obvious thing was to read that library too. It was much smaller then. The task now would be impossible in eight years. There was no catalogue. The books were read in order as they came from the shelf. But this reading was a disturbance of more serious work. Matthew Arnold, Ruskin, Walter Pater, Walter Bagehot, Renan, and Sainte Beuve must bear the chief blame. It will be remarked that these were journalists all, save one, and that exception only when he wrote poetry. It was a journalist I aspired to be.

The danger of reading is that it engenders the desire to write, even if one has nothing to say. I do not remember the time when it was not my habit to string words together. By long practice I have learned to articulate sentences : I have never been able to animate them by the silver cord of life. The first money I earned was with my young pen. The prize was a dollar. The theme was education, a subject upon which I have been writing ever since with less finality of opinion than I then enjoyed. The next considerable prize was five hundred dollars for a presentation of the argument in favour of an unpopular cause. There was a like amount for the contrary argument, and it was hinted darkly that I

had won both. The suggestion was free from malice :
it was merely a recognition of that fatal capacity to
see the paradox of things, that is, both sides of
a subject at the same time.

I never was a student. I never became a scholar.
Even my professional studies were perfunctory. The
mother was right. I was spoiled by reading. Worse
still, I had learned too well her lesson that scholastic
achievement was only a means in life and not life
itself. I was too careful to learn no more than the
academic law demanded, and I learned that little too
easily. Only once did I miscalculate. Of sixty-seven
major examinations I failed in one only. In nearly all
others I escaped notice in the large middle average.

There was too much in life, and life was too short.
Whole areas I avoided by deliberate choice. To think
mathematically or even to learn the symbols was for
me only a little less preposterous than an attempt to
learn the signs which the deaf and dumb employ
when they converse. Science was only a series of
categories. A fossil in a rock was a revelation which
was not enlarged by knowing that it was a *trilobite*.
I yield to no one in my admiration of the moon in
the heavens, but I only recently learned why it looks
different on successive nights. So far as I could
observe, "scientists" of those days were like carpenters
working at a trade, and I had no intention of
becoming a carpenter, or a scientist either. I had
escaped from that.

One important reservation I should make. I
learned to use the microscope, when that instrument

was yet a mystery; but I used it like a pair of spectacles, to examine a world inaccessible to the unaided eye. And one further explanation should be made. When I thought it prudent to begin the practice of medicine, I went to London and lived in the Whitechapel Road beside the London Hospital. After a year I emerged from the Royal College of Surgeons and the Royal College of Physicians with their stamps upon me. Henceforth there was no pontiff in the profession whom I was not authorized to contradict. But I emerged a lean and broken wretch : it required the twelve days of the return voyage to restore me.

Le moi est haissable; and yet the picture of that life must not be marred by lack of a few additional strokes. All students in those days lived on the same level. If one had money, he was careful to conceal it, lest he be held in contempt for enjoying an unfair advantage. In the richer families an initial fund would be provided sufficient for the eldest boy. He in turn would pass it on year by year to the next candidate. In some cases three boys would be educated from the fund in twelve years; and in the end the youngest would repay it to the father for his old age. Less fortunate aspirants would accumulate enough for one year at least. In the summer, work was always to be found with survey or exploration parties, and even a whole year might be spent in those employments. A person with a taste for private teaching could earn enough in an hour to keep him for the day. By skill and industry, following a sound preliminary training, a student could condense into six years the courses in Arts and Medicine which nominally required eight.

When I entered the University, my capital was three hundred dollars. But far in the background was the certainty that the Master's reserve fund was always at the disposal of his six sons. At Christmas the Master's wife sent a bank-note. There was no need. I had discovered that the pen is a useful tool. I have that same note yet, but the bank has long since gone out of existence. One may be over-thrifty. When I emerged from the University, after having passed through the Faculties of Arts and Medicine, I owed nothing and had 1200 dollars saved by the movement of that little pen, and by the traditional art of teaching. Heine has truly said, "I thought I never could bear it; I did bear it; only do not ask me how." There was one merit in all this labour. I learned to sleep without appearing to be asleep, and by that gift was spared many a useless lecture. But we did not live meanly. From the first I had a companion, yet inseparable. By a deliberate act of daring challenge against the future, we bought a small piano and a Turkish rug. They are yet at Orwell. For many years he would awaken me at the proper time by striking a chord on the piano. That chord is yet hateful to me. When now I am sleepless, I strike that chord.

XVII

HER HUMANITY

In the whole district of Orwell with a hundred families there were only three poor persons. The one was an old man who suffered from a shaking palsy; the second was a widow with seven small children; the third was a lame woman who lived alone. There was no public provision for their support, but they were not left in want. The Master's wife appointed herself guardian of the two women, and me her deputy.

On New Year's day, and at two other times every year, I was entrusted with a horse and vehicle, and given a roving commission to the neighbours in search of provision. It was a hateful task, only a little less hateful than begging one's own bread. The only other trial equally hard was the compulsion to say the grace before meat. After one of these excursions I obtained a happy deliverance. The eldest daughter of the widow had become a well grown girl. When I arrived with my spoil so hardly won, she greeted me with honest tears of mortification, reproached me for inflicting upon them the stigma of charity, and recommended me with injurious words to mind my own business.

The other recipient was known as Peggy *crupaidh*, to distinguish her from the miller's wife, who, as she

boasted, "walked upright in the image of her maker."
This woman was reputed to be a miser, as I was
frequently informed by astute persons whom I
solicited on her behalf. Certainly, when she died a
box was found beneath her bed, and when it was
opened with a key which she carried upon a string
about her neck, it contained a store of ancient coins.
She had a little flock of sheep, and the neighbours
would winter them for her. In the spring they were
shorn; the wool was returned to her; and the offspring
were clipped in the ears with her mark. On every
farm "Peggy's sheep" were to be found and by some
miracle they always bore twin lambs. When she died
her nearest relation suddenly appeared, and collected
them with punctilious care.

The house in which she lived was the last of its
kind, built of logs, with a roof of boards, with an
open fireplace, and a cat-and-clay chimney. When
the house was no longer habitable, that was the
guardian's great hour. She would have a new one
built. But the old house was upon land to which
Peggy had no title. The new house therefore would
become the property of the owner of the land.

The Master, with his fine unconcern of earthly
possessions, drew up a paper of release, which he
presented to the owner for signature. To his astonishment, the man quite properly refused "to give a deed"
to any part of his land. Worse still, the horrid
rumour spread that this guardian of the poor was
attempting to secure for herself the reversion of both
house and land at the woman's death. In the end

the house was built on the "King's highway," whence in due time it was promptly removed by the man who had acquired the coins and the sheep.

In the worst moment of the tragedy a miracle happened. Peggy was bewailing her fate. She would go to the poor-house. The Master protested that she would have the best room in his house. I saw our little parlour with the carpet, the marble table, the hair-cloth chairs, the sofa, the elaborate stove, the organ, abandoned to this old woman; for even at that early age I was aware that he was capable of any such sacrifice. His wife had another opinion, but said nothing. They were sitting by an open window. Suddenly in the outer air arose the clear voice of a young child :

> Blessed is he that wisely doth
> The poor man's case consider;
> For when the time of trouble is,
> The Lord will him deliver.

The old woman fell upon her crooked knees. "Who but the Lord put those words in the mouth of the child ? " she exclaimed. It must have been so. He was too young to have acquired the message by earthly agency; impossible that he should have delivered it at a moment so opportune. All discussion was at an end. The house was built.

An elder brother had remarkable skill in the use of his knife. He could carve a watch chain from a long piece of wood. One thing the young child earnestly desired, a delicately sharpened peg to replace a fallen button. The elder one promised him the treasure on one condition. He must learn the words of the psalm, and repeat them at the open window. The terms of the agreement were promptly observed.

It was more than forty years before I learned the source of the inspiration. My informant was the young child himself, who now was in command of a brigade of sappers, as we sat together one long winter night, talking of old things in the house of a Prussian cavalry officer in Deutz, which is beyond the Rhine. On our return we agreed after much debate to disclose the truth to the Master's wife.

"I knew very well you were at some kind of mischief," she admitted; "but your father was pleased; and the house was built."

We never were convinced that she was animated by the abstract spirit of charity alone. She would send a child trudging through the snow with a basket of eggs, fresh butter, biscuits, and apples to the Minister's wife, and to other persons who had no need or desire for gifts. We now suspect she had made the discovery that the bestowal of favours is the most subtle domination and the easiest way to its achievement. One who accepts charity has surrendered freedom, becomes a dependent, and is transformed, as a wolf is changed into a domestic animal. It is quite true that charity may cover the sin of pride.

But in the visitation of the sick her heart was pure. The doctor had no part in the life of the community. The women were their own doctors, and she had an intuitive skill which she developed by experience. Her peculiar gift was the treatment of the *weed*. Nomenclature of disease is not one of the excellencies of the Gaelic tongue, and this term is used indifferently to describe a swelling on a horse's leg due to long standing in the stall, or a condition of lassitude prevalent in nursing women. But as all women in those days were almost continuously subject to that strain, it is probable that the *weed* signified a state of specific neurasthenia. It was well known that some men were subject to it. Indeed, a distinguished professor has affirmed that towards the spring of the year he himself is afflicted with a kind of mental *weed*, which he attributes to the continuous nursing which the modern student demands. Her remedy was the same as Martin Luther employed when he was afflicted by the sight of devils, a draught of strong sweet liquor. But this prescription was merely a placebo. She would send the woman to the woods in search of a herb of extreme rarity. The herb was never found; but the walk in the woods in the spring air and sunshine always completed the cure.

For every ill there was a remedy. The art of dentistry was practised by the blacksmith. His sole instrument was a powerful "key," made by his own hands, which he kept in his farrier's box. By it the most obstinate tooth could be extracted. If the jaw-bone was fractured that was the fault of the patient, not of the operator. But the extraction of a tooth in those days was as rare a catastrophe as the loss of an arm or a leg. The coarse tooth-brush had not begun

its deadly work with children. Ten children had been
born in the house before a doctor was known to enter,
save once for the rite of vaccination and upon one
other occasion beyond my memory. Of this ancient
visit I had a strange reminder one night, when I was
called away from this writing by a venerable friend
to his apartment which had in it many old and
beautiful things.

The heating of his room was reinforced,
unnecessarily as I thought, by a handsome stove. This
stove had been made in Glasgow, and at one time
belonged to Dr. Kaye of Georgetown, a thousand
miles from Montreal. It was this Dr. Kaye who
attended the Master's wife seventy-five years ago.
He died in 1891, at the age of 92 years. The Master
went on his horse fifteen miles to summon him, and
the two came riding back together, the doctor having
arisen from the same stove by which I sat seventy
years afterwards.

To be obliged to take "doctor's medicine" was
a sign of the end; "to fall into the doctor's hands"
a living calamity. The mere suggestion of "a hospital"
filled her with an alarm that was almost terror; mal-
treatment was her word. And yet one autumn near
the end of her life, she was persuaded to enter the
Island Hospital to be cured of a cough which had
defied wild cherry bark, flax-seed, slippery elm, and
neat's-foot oil. She was cured instantly and liked the
place so well, that she remained all winter.

The nurses too were kind, but "untruthful."
They would not inform her fully of all that passed

within the walls; they would evade her enquiries or even mislead. This "falsehood" she considered was a deliberate part of their training, since no amount of "questioning" on her part could elicit the details of a case in which she was interested. Indeed a patient had died, and she was not promptly informed of the sad event. She left the hospital as a sign of protest.

Two things astonished the Master's wife : her own continual mildness, and the truculence of others. She never, so far as she was aware, gave offence to anyone, and yet offence would be taken. A servant whom she urged to remember the injunction "servants obey your master," fell into a passion, and would not have the Scripture put upon her; another would not be put in mind of hell, even if she did not choose to reveal the name of the young man who had walked home with her. For a young woman, especially a niece, to "toss her head" and remain silent was worse than revolt, since it put a stop to further discussion.

The truth is, she had an immense curiosity about life, which developed into a love of gossip. She would not "question" a person, but she would contrive to be told; and it was a grievance if information were withheld of such important matters as sickness and death, of an absconding man or a levanting wife, and especially of the imminence of an illegitimate child. When workmen were engaged upon the place she would make an early round and gather up the news they had acquired during the night. In exchange, there was always a surreptitious drink. But the reticence and understatement of the Highlander was a sore trial to her.

Neil Gillis, that most honest and best carpenter, was one of these. He could make the replica of a Chippendale chair or replace sills under an old barn with equal perfection. I consulted him upon the difficult problem of repairing a barn or building a new one. He regarded me with the appraising eye of a life insurance examiner; then he scrutinized the barn.

"The trouble is," he said, "a man might live longer than his building." Repairs would last a certain time; but in the unfortunate event of one living too long, one might find one's self without a barn, compelled to build a new one in an enfeebled old age. He rarely spoke, and yet one could sit by the hour and watch him work, in placid enjoyment. Watching another man work is the most delicate form of exercise.

Neil had a neighbour, a distant relative of her own, who was very sick. When he came to work in the morning, she asked him :

"Did you hear how David is ? "

"Yes ma'am."

"When did you hear ? "

"Last night."

"Perhaps you saw him ? "

"Yes, ma'am."

"At what time ? "

"Eight."

"And how was he ? "

"Pretty slack." I myself had seen the man an hour earlier; he was then unconscious and died in the night.

It was a pretty game to conceal these events from her, and watch her ingenuity in discovering them. But she could not understand our stupid lack of interest in life. We were like persons in another sphere, who could deliberately refrain from reading the Court Circular in the *Morning Post*.

To the end of her days she affected to believe that the Master was yet alive, and with sure effect made veiled and dark reference to his example and authority against her children, as the supreme law of the household, long after the time when by age at least they might be assumed to have "a will of their own." The vague suggestion, that he being dead yet speaketh, was her final weapon. It is quite true that every year on the anniversary of his death which falls on July 4th, but at no other time, an inexplicable visitant makes a transient appearance by night in the room in which he was transformed. The phenomenon has been amply tested.

One example, however, will serve to demonstrate the less esoteric reality of his presence. He sat on a chair with his feet firmly and evenly placed upon the floor. Not many years ago a man came to see me in great distress. His son had been convicted of the murder of his wife, and was undergoing the punishment of fifteen years in prison. The man came as soon as he heard I had arrived, driving fifteen miles over the bad spring roads. He sat on the chair precisely as the Master would, and I knew him for a worthy man. So strong was the impression, I took a new and sudden interest in him.

The trial and conviction was an event of the previous year. The counsel for the defence, a very old friend, since Chief-Justice, came to see me at the end of the first day. The case turned upon the post-mortem appearance of the body. The woman had been found hanged, and there were certain dis-coloured spots on the neck, which it was contended were caused by the man's fingers and not by the rope. The charge was that he had strangled his wife, and then suspended her. It was all surmise; there was no evidence.

I had been for a long time professor of pathology, when it was part of my business to make autopsies, and determine the cause of death. In addition I had acquired a special experience in such cases, for I had performed autopsies upon the bodies of thirteen persons who had been judicially hanged, one of whom was a woman. Indeed, she and her accomplice were hanged on the one scaffold at the same moment. I was asked to give expert evidence; but, unfortunately for the prisoner, I had just lost by accident the use of an eye, and was still wearing bandages. To our astonishment the man was convicted of the crime, as we felt sure, unjustly.

When I recovered enough vision. I obtained the official report of the trial, and could find no medical evidence of the man's guilt. I submitted the record to two other persons even more expert than myself, and they agreed. Still more, one of these, Dr. J. G.

Adami, afterwards vice-chancellor of Liverpool University, and at that time the greatest authority upon such cases, discovered unexpected technical proof in the evidence itself that the woman had committed suicide. In proper form the whole case was put before the Minister of Justice, and it was to ascertain what progress was being made that the convict's father came to see me. I had never seen him before, but his manner of sitting on the chair reminded me of the Master, and the case had now an element of personal interest. This interest was probably heightened by the Master's wife's profound assurance of the prisoner's guilt, and by her suggestion that I would do better to mind my own business. She had heard things about the man which she would not disclose. Apparently they were not very delicate, and she was never known to utter an indelicate word.

In due course, the prisoner was released. Public passion had calmed, and the satisfaction was so general that the two local members of parliament thought well to take credit for his freedom, and so provided me with a ready defence against her blame. It also provided her with a grievance against "the politicians" in that they assumed credit which she was well aware should have come to "one of her own."

When he came out of prison, I went to see him secretly. He was doing his best to restore the ruin that had fallen upon his farm in his absence. The day was hot, and the farm was poor. He had been comfortable in prison; he had worked on the prison farm, and did not appear to find much difference upon his own. He was not very glad to see me, and I began to suspect that she may have been right in her injunction, that I should have minded my own business.

His two little sisters, without a word, went to the woods, and gathered a basket of raspberries as their tribute. I brought them home and we had them for dinner. She praised them without reserve. Through innocence on the part of the driver she soon discovered the source of the fruit. She took to her bed on the pretext that she had been poisoned. Some years afterwards the released prisoner married again. I asked her what kind of a woman he had taken to wife.

"A woman of courage," she said. "He will murder her too, and it will serve her right. You will not get him out of gaol the second time."

XVIII

THE TWO HORSES

The Master's wife, in marked contrast with her benevolence, courage, and energy within the family, was shy in presence of strangers, timid in face of the mysterious forces of the world. In strange contrast, too, with her own shyness, timidity, and charity were her bold and biting judgements of persons without the family, especially of women. She judged them by her own standard of propriety. If a woman met with calamity in departing from that standard; if she engaged in a conversation where men were present, especially if she laughed aloud and exposed her teeth, dressed unseemly, washed or combed her hair where she might be seen, danced in a public place, went into the sea to bathe or swim, entered a boat or canoe, or in short indulged in violent pleasure of any kind — misfortune, even death, "served her right."

And yet she could not look upon pain. To pain in herself she seemed insensible. She would not remove a splinter from a child's foot; the operation was entrusted to an elder child. The sight of blood made her faint. The simple surgery which the Master might perform upon the "bealed" finger of a child filled her with anguish. The familiar surgery of the farm was her especial abhorrence. The operator was the one person of the year who was denied the hospitality of the house. Animals must be killed, but they must be killed without her knowledge.

There was always a dog in the house, and she made much of the fierceness of the beast. In the Master's absence upon his official visits, she was often left alone with her little children in that secluded house with only the dog for protection. Late in the night, a drunken tramp would come for shelter, and that was a night of terror. She would secretly incite the dog to fierceness, and assemble the children in the most remote and secure room, where all spent the dark hours in deadly fear of assault and in the more immediate fear lest the man might burn down the house. Later in life, when she lived much alone, she had for companion a proper dog, a Newfoundland, as big as a well grown calf. Any visitor who entered the house, man or woman, he would seize by the hand with gentle firmness, and retain until he was ordered to release by an authorized person. This faithful creature was poisoned by a distant neighbour, and she spent many years in discovering the poisoner. For the rest of her life she watched with slow delight the decadence of him and his family into distress.

Her fondness for all animals was inherited, and transmitted. It was more than a feeling of kindness; it was a passion. She would loose a tied beast out of sheer pity, although it was in no way uncomfortable, and would be sure to do harm to itself or to the crops. She imputed to it her own feelings in similar circumstances.

On a journey to the town, she walked up Tea Hill. Never in her life had she allowed a horse to draw a loaded carriage up that incredible mountain. The ascent was a gentle slope nearly half-a-mile long and reached a point 198 feet above the level of the sea, as she proved by an aneroid barometer. When she first made the ascent in a motor-car, she could hardly be restrained from her immemorial practice of walking up the hill. But she was somewhat reconciled to that method of conveyance : "It saved the horses." Only twice did she enter a motor-car. She thought it an unsafe and licentious way of travelling.

This excessive care of horses was a trial to her family. A child, or herself, might go afoot an a journey of five miles rather than "take a horse out of the stable." When we were old enough to have horses of our own, she exercised the usual oversight. "Your beast is warm," was her invariable comment, as one returned from driving; and if there were no obvious sign of warmth, she would slip her hand under the collar. "Dry under the collar" was the sign of a merciful man.

When we took her driving, we strove to excel by never going faster than a walk. At length she would say, "You might trot a little here; it is on the level." If she ever urged a horse to trot, she would explain to him that it was down hill. She approved of the parish priest, afterwards Bishop, who always employed towards his horse the formula : Get up, please. One granddaughter had her own horse, but there was always abundant reasons why she could

not go riding : the day was too hot; it looked like
rain; or finally the creature's legs were too slender
to support so heavy a child. A powerful grey horse
ran away with a boy of the new generation, and might
have killed him. When the horse galloped home
with a broken and empty carriage, her sympathy was
all for the horse, and her blame for the boy when he
came toiling home.

"Are you not afraid of what your father will
say ? " she asked of him.

"Yes — to the horse." It came as a shock to her
that a boy might have a right to his life, which a
horse was bound to respect.

She reckoned the date of events by the age of her
children, and epochs by the life span of a horse. She
remembered their names, knew their pedigree and
personal history, and would recall the feats of
strength, speed, and endurance they had performed.
Her later years were comforted by two horses known
as Gipsy I, and Gipsy II. She gave to them her final
love of animals. Early one summer morning I arrived
from the east at Grand Metis, which is the junction
for Little Metis, a resort on the south shore of the St.
Lawrence. There was an hour's wait for the train
from New York, by which Newell Dwight Hillis,
pastor of Plymouth Church, an old friend, was to
arrive. In a field was a small black Canadian pony,
and a profitable hour was spent in talking with her.
When Dr. Hillis arrived, we continued the
conversation. A knowledge of horses was another
of his accomplishments. The horse was bought and

sent to Orwell. The Master's wife admitted that she had seen as perfect a head, as beautiful a neck, as comely a body, as shapely a set of legs, as sound hoofs, and as dainty a skin; but she declared she had never before discovered all those excellencies assembled in one single animal. To her was given the natural right of bestowing a name.

"She can be called nothing else but Gipsy," she said.

After further years I was at Truro in Nova Scotia, "stormstayed" for the night, and to pass the time went to see a moving-picture performance. The scene depicted a journey up the Rhine, showing castles, vineyards, gardens. At one spot a man on a black horse rode down to the river. As the horse drank, it pawed the water, and the drops made rainbows in the sun. The horse was like Gipsy.

Again, in the winter of 1915, it was part of my business in an English village to draw 37 horses for a Field Ambulance proceeding to France. I spied another Gipsy and marked her for my own, with the name of Gipsy II. She was an exact replica, but on a much larger scale, evidently a lady's carriage horse, but now in the class, light draught for gun team. At the first water she pawed with her powerful foot. She was the horse of the picture, and even in the darkest hours of the war the vision never left me. I was certain that I should water Gipsy II in the Rhine. I did, the day after Christmas, 1918, on the further bank. She pawed the water with her foot, and the drops shone in the pale winter light. The brother who had been with me at Truro was with me on the Rhine, and can testify that the vision came true. She, too, arrived at Orwell for her final home.

When Lord Byng came to Orwell, he desired to make an inspection of this horse which he had once inspected in Reninghelst. The parade state was increased by the presence of Tommy, the brother's horse, which he had selected at Valcartier in 1914, rode to the Rhine, and brought back to Orwell. One of Lord Byng's young men averred that he recognized Gipsy as a carriage horse that once belonged to a lady in England. The English women held nothing back.

The Master's wife seldom rode after her marriage, but her saddle is still extant. The Master's saddle was stolen. She always hinted that she knew the one who stole it. She first felt the warmth of a horse when she was ten years old. An aunt had come, and was put to sleep with the girl. In the night she awoke with a feeling of something strange. She could not withdraw her hand from the grasp of the old woman. The woman was dead. In the morning the child was sent on horseback to convey the intelligence and to carry in a bundle the woman's few belongings. As a reward, she was given a blanket that had come from Scotland. When she married, the blanket was left in the old house. It passed through various hands, but she "kept her eye on it," and it was forty years before she retrieved it for her own. She quilted it into a "comforter," bestowed it upon her daughter who in turn gave it as a marriage portion to her own. In the spare room a visitor may yet sleep in comfort beneath that old blanket.

The Master's wife would never relate the experience of her life. In itself it was too insignificant. She would never elevate an incident to the dignity of a separate narration. If used at all, it was merely to enforce the present theme. A single question would bring down the whole fabric of her remembrance, and she took refuge in silence. There was no use in talking to people who were interested in the trivial incident of a young girl awakening in the night to find her hand in the grasp of a dead woman, when the real object of conversation was the avarice of persons who would keep a blanket that did not belong to them, or the enormity of riding a horse until the beast was warm.

The Master rode with ease and grace, and in the visitation of schools would make a journey that kept him in the saddle long hours and long miles. From him his sons learned to ride as birds learn to fly. The horses were small, but strong from their daily work, and could do forty miles as a matter of course.

In time of war this early gift was the first I had to offer. At the age of seventeen I acquired from a neighbour the use of a Kentucky mare, and from that violent beast learned all that is to be known of the mastery of a horse. She was four years old before she felt a bit, and would crush a boy to death if he entered her stall. Her owner alone at first was allowed to saddle and bridle her. Her procedure after one had mounted was to rear twice and throw herself backward on the ground. To free one's self and mount before she was up required some alacrity. Then she would bolt for the open sea; but there was a stretch of sand into which she could be guided deeper and deeper as her strength failed until she came to rest.

Some years later, I was spending a summer in western New York, and there fell in with a soldier who had ridden through the Civil War. He taught me style. Again I had a chance to ride with a French Army officer; and last of all I completed the instruction with a professional riding master. When war broke out, I remembered this old art as a compensation for advancing age. I went to Toronto where an old friend, Colonel Fotheringham, had begun a course of instruction for newly commissoned officers in foot-drill, tactics, and equitation. For the trials, horses were brought in, and I gave the sergeant a dollar for the worst, a procedure so reverse that it could not be called improper. He assigned to me a horse called "The Devil." The name by the horse and the pay by the sergeant were honestly earned. I gained the certificate. On my return to Montreal I was detailed for duty as instructor in equitation, and of the class of fifty only one failed to pass. They presented me with a watch somewhat humorously inscribed. That was the only exploit of my life in which the Master's wife appeared to take any pride.

Gipsy II still lives, happy in herself and a cause of happiness in others. She has already taught six children to walk, by allowing her foreleg to be used for their support. But "little Gipsy" is gone. In time she developed an emphysema of the lungs, with painful laboured breathing, commonly called "the heaves." Her life was near the end. I was obliged to make a visit to Newfoundland to advise the government upon a question of plant pathology with which I was familiar. At Sydney I gained courage to pronounce sentence, and sent a telegram to my brother. When I returned, Gipsy was part of the hillside, and posted in her stall was a sonnet which he had made in expiation of the act and in remembrance of her. It was entitled, "At an unmarked Mound" :

Dust unto dust ! Nay, shallow laid, she stirs
    I guess, when springtime and the streamlets call
    Even though, the while, her ever-thickening pall
Is wrought by the deft needles of the firs.
Ashes to ashes : still I fancy hers
    Must glow if any human breath at all
    Shall breathe upon them, though the winter fall
A fathom deep, and doubly sure inters.

Faint as she whinnies in this studied rhyme,
    Yet if a human child but shed a tear
    For her, she rises, answering tears with mirth,
To roam through pastures green the livelong year;
    So she lives on, till, in a little time,
    All living turns to earth : earth unto earth.

XIX

THE MUSICIANS

THE Master was also a good musician. He sang in a voice that was true, rich, and strong. He had sufficient skill in technique to set down in musical notation any tune he heard sung. He had a repertory that was large but not varied, and he was continually extending it. On every journey when he was Inspector of Schools he would bring home a new song. The parish house of the priests was a fertile field, but he would amend their hymns and songs to bring them into conformity with his own established doctrine. In a description of heaven he would substitute "brightness" for "sunshine." With his more precise information he was aware that the heavenly "city had no need of the sun."

He performed on no instrument. His sole appliance was a "pitchpipe," that belonged to his *maestro*, an American musician, named Tyson. Later, he had a tuning-fork which he carried in his waist-coat pocket, and bit between his teeth to elicit the sound. The pitch-pipe was a whistle, in section two inches square and about a foot long; it had a plunger marked with the notes; and the complete scale could be played by successive thrusts or withdrawal of this plunger. Indeed with skill one could produce any tune that lay within the compass of eight notes. Even the chanter of the bag-pipes does not cover a greater range.

The Master never allowed his love of music to lead him into excess. There was an organ in the house, and — much later — a piano. The "new Minister's" wife played very well, and would accompany him. At times a gifted colporteur, an agent for books, lightning rods, or fruit trees would come. Then there was a concert, and their return was eagerly looked for. Like all persons with a gift, the Master thought his own gift was of great educational advantage to others. He taught music in his school, and when he became Inspector of 180 schools he implanted his musical ideas in a wide field.

It was in no perfunctory way he taught music. He transcribed the scores on sheets large enough to be read by a class of forty persons. These sheets were rolls of wall paper. He ruled the staffs on the reverse side, and marked the notes with a piece of cork dipped in black ink; the sharps, flats, and clefs were done in red with a quill pen. Modern musicians who have had the privilege of examining these simple manuscripts made by the Master then long since dead, were astonished at their perfection, although they did not inspect them with that curiosity with which anthropologists regard hieroglyphics on the walls of a cave.

One of these musicians, a soprano from the Metropolitan Opera in New York, who spent three summers at Orwell, sang all these forgotten scores with perfect understanding. An old neighbour, who happened to be present, removed his coat, and in his white shirt lay down upon a couch. When the music finished, he arose in such bewilderment as Lazarus must have shown. He affected to have been dead and in heaven. The singer said that was the most profound and subtle praise she had received, in a distinguished European and American career. She too is now dead.

Musical instruments were not held in favour. One young man who performed very well on the bag-pipes abandoned the practice at the time of his conversion; and to prove his sincerity destroyed the instrument which he had created with his own hands. The violin was unknown, except among the Irish. It was considered a dissolute instrument. The performer on the violin always strove to enforce the rhythm by trampling with his feet to give the effect of drums. He required a firm seat, a level and hard floor. If the floor were not level he would choose the highest corner. It had happened that some mischievous boys poured water by the wall of the room, which ran down to the lowest level and was trampled into a spray which soon silenced the strings.

In that Island there are no stones, unless they are quarried with great labour from the earth, and these are all red sandstone. There was — and is yet — a single boulder in a field, the last of the glacial drift; but it was believed to have fallen from heaven. In a spirit of reckless pride I imported a white stone for

a doorstep; "a tall man could lie upon it." Many
visitors came to view the wonder. Amongst the
visitors was Pat Bolger, the last of the violinists, who
discerned at once the essential utility of the stone.
He brought his fiddle, and played a long composition
of his own to his entire satisfaction. The resonant
stone gave the effect of a complete orchestra.

The work was entitled, *The Arkansaw Traveller.*
It was like all of Rimsky-Korsakoff's, a medley of
popular airs; but this musician, also like the great
Russian, would play the tune as it is commonly
played, and then embellish it with the riches of his
own inner imagination. He made his own fiddle.
An old gaol had been pulled down — quite officially
— and yielded from the wainscot fir wood which
had been in place for a hundred years. From this
wood he made a fiddle for me at a cost of three
dollars.

This same Pat Bolger in later years enlivened
many a slow railway journey. He would play the
fiddle, and any one who liked might dance in the
aisle. In passing the stations of Highland settlements
he would play derisory tunes. It often happened that
there was a Highlander on the train, who had brought
with him his bag-pipes to console himself on the slow
journey, and he would remember tunes equally
irritating as he passed through an Irish settlement.
There was some interest in music in those days.

This Pat Bolger was the protagonist of the classical
school. Tradition was his guide; but the tradition
did not extend much further back than his own

experience. The protagonist of the romantic school in music, and poetry, too, was Donald *beag*, a little man. His canon was that the distinguishing mark of poetry was tune; he denied that movement alone was the test of music. Indeed, he would not admit a divorce between the two modes. If the poet could not confine his thought within the bounds of meter and rhythm, then he had "better take to the pulpit." He was quite ready to put any verse to the test of his own singing voice. If it would sing, it obeyed the inherent law of poetry : if not, it might be a sermon; he was not sure; he was no judge of sermons. He was deaf to that form of expression; his ear was for poetry and music alone. He called the birds to be his witness and authority.

This Donald *beag* was a free man from the day he left "the tail of the Greenock bank." He was reputed to have, or to have had, seven wives, and at various times to have owned three well stocked farms. But now, he was "not troubled wi' weemen, not troubled wi' farms, not troubled wi' horses, not troubled wi' aething." His only tools were an ax and a heavy hoe. His trade was clearing land of stumps. He would build a pile as if it were a cathedral, and then set it on fire. He worked for us many summers. His wage was a dollar a day. He was allowed twenty-five cents for subsistence, and he made for himself a casual sleeping shelter in the woods. In the morning he stripped himself to the waist, worked all day, and in the evening, stripped himself completely and plunged into the cold stream.

He was not overpaid, although he spent much of the time in musical criticism of Pat Bolger. And yet the violinist could not keep away. He would bring his fiddle to the woods, and play traditional airs and compositions of his own, which had been well received "at a theatre in Boston."

These two were at eternal enmity. They were always talking about different aspects of the same thing, each accusing the other of holding opinions that were peculiar to himself when in reality they were common to both. In addition, there was the inevitable enmity between the talker and the doer, between the theorist and the performer. Failure to apprehend the argument lay in the intellectual stupidity of the musician. When the quality of the performance was attacked, the musician attributed any defect in his cadence to the absence of a firm footing whereon he might trample with his feet. At the moment of my approach he was making the final taunt :

"It is classical music you want ! "

"It is good music I want. Classical music played by you is bad as any other." Then on sudden reflection he added, "Good music does bad to a bad mind : bad music makes a bad mind worse. That is all there is to it." To make this judgement universal he added, "That is true also of pictures : it is not true of writing. The papers your brother sends you from Boston are good for you : the Bible is good for both of us."

"What is good and bad, Donald ? "

"A man may be good in the sight of God, and yet love bad music. Look at yourself. But he cannot love bad writing. A man may be bad in the sight of God, and yet love good music; but it does him only harm. Look at me. Not one of us is perfect."

This much I heard before the two protagonists were aware that I had come upon the scene. An honest workman is never embarrassed when he is found idle. He is merely resting for a greater effort. I was even offered a place by the fire.

"We are disputing about music," Pat Bolger said, with the easy confidence of an educated man who is not drawing pay for work.

"We are not disputing; I am explaining music to him." I asked that I be allowed to share in the process.

The spot was in a slight valley traversed by the stream. A timber bridge carried the road across. The stream for a space and moment was broad and still, and then tumbled over stones or fled along the gravelly bottom between the trees on either bank.

"Play me the music of the stream," the little man said : "you cannot do it," A kingfisher came flashing up from the sea, and screamed as he discovered us.

"Play me that," he repeated. A sentinel crow cried three times from his perch. "Play me that." Here was the old controversy between the realist and the symbolist, between Sousa, Strauss, and Stravinsky on the one hand, Debussy on the other; between the two elements at strife in the single mind of Wagner, and even of Mozart himself.

The afternoon lay long before us. Pat Bolger sought from his own wide experience — for he had been in Boston — to justify his theory of natural sounds in music. He had heard a band play a piece called *Afternoon at Coney Island*, in which one could hear the train roar and the whistle scream and the brakes squeal. He thought it admirable.

"I can still hear that train," was his final defence.

"If it is a railway train you want to hear; go up the stream to the station. Listen for yourself, and do not bother making music or remembering what you heard in Boston." A bird sang a few notes of a broken melody.

"Is yonder bird describing something? Is he calling to your mind what you felt in Boston or anywhere else? No, Pat. Music is a present pleasure. It is itself."

The musician fell back for argument to his fiddle. He played a tune which always won him favour at a "tea-party." He saw again the booth of leaves with the sunlight filtering through upon the white boards; he heard the feet of the dancers, and possibly the coppers each partner paid jingling in his pocket as he himself swayed to the tune.

"There is music you can dance to," he declared in triumph.

"With my feet — yes. Does it make the heart dance in my breast, or the tears sparkle in my eyes? Can you make music that goes upon its own legs? Give me that machine," he cried in sudden passion.

Donald *beag* took the fiddle and stood up. He played eight bars, then the same eight bars at a higher pitch; and yet again in the original key but in the next octave above. By four bar passages he descended gently into the opening quietness, drawing the bow across the strings half way down towards the finger-board with a light quivering sound :

"There now; there is music and movement for you; and yet the Woman is dead."

He in turn was now the musician. He paused for a moment whilst he fingered the keys and brought the tune of the strings to his taste. Then drawing the bow across close to the bridge, he made the fiddle scream out a tormenting dance of wild creatures. Half naked, grimy with smoke, with his bare feet, whilst the fire blazed, he kept the time, first with heavy gambols like the pig in the children's book, then with the slow struttings of some lascivious bird, and then like a little gnome at a speed that was nothing short of ecstasy. He was not himself; he was another person. In Pat's eyes was a sudden flame of jealous wonder. He leaped up, but barely caught his beloved fiddle before it was flung in the fire. With a passionate imprecation he turned and disappeared in the woods.

"A fool — yes : damned — no; not yet," Donald said in lament and thankfulness. He put out his hand for the fiddle, but it was gone.

"But Pat is right, half right. Like Michal, Saul's daughter, he despised me in his heart, and well he might. I despise myself. I am no better than that poor German man."

He put out his hand again for the fiddle, but it was gone. In default, he uttered clear coherent sounds that were none other than the cries and calls to *Tannhauser* to come to the mountains of fleshly delight.

"Where did you learn to make music ? " I made bold to ask.

"I played second for the Orchestral Society in St. Andrew's Hall in Grenville Street. It was the Manns himself who once led me."

"Why did you stop playing ? "

"I was saying things on the fiddle for which they would put me in gaol if only they understood what I was saying. But there is one who understands, the searcher of hearts, and hell is his prison. When I was converted, I sold the fiddle and bought liquor. From that day until this I have touched neither the one nor the other." He held out his hand with a gesture that was final and defiant.

"I shall be leaving you," he said. "The few shillings coming to me you will give to Janet who lodged me. They say she killed her man; but she is not immoral whatever. It is myself should know."

"Have I not been kind to you ? " I asked in fear lest I may have failed in my duty to one of these little ones.

"Kind — yes. We are friends. It is not that." He lowered his voice to a whisper. "Last night I heard the Woman calling me. I am one of the goats."

With this dark saying he too turned and was lost to me in the woods forever.

The fire had died down, and I made my way up the stream. In the summer air sound carries far. The Master's wife then near the end of her days had been attracted to the spot. I encountered her in an open space, with an air of detachment as if she were merely picking a few raspberries for the flavour or considering a brood of young partridges.

"I think Julia is coming too," was all she said.

This was the singer with the soprano voice from the Metropolitan Opera. She had arrived the previous day to spend the remainder of this, the third summer. Down the ravine, and filling the evening heavens, came her voice. It was from *Solveig's* song, the Woman singing as she spins in the sunshine before her cottage door, yearning for *Peer Gynt*, and breaking the melody to call her goats from the hills. In such a voice this cry of at least thirty notes in the major mode and triple time also carries far. This was really the call to the goats Donald *beag* had heard the evening before; but he was determined that he should save his soul alive. He had long since renounced all. We rested on a newly cut log, the three of us.

"Pat Bolger would do better to keep out of the woods with his wild fiddling," the elder woman said; "he will give the place a bad name."

"He played *The Death of Aase* very well," the singer protested mildly, but with professional respect. She repeated the tune.

"There is no harm in that," the other replied.

"And *Anitra's Dance* was well done."

"He might better be at his work; he does little enough for what he is paid."

"But where did he learn to sing my own *Tannhauser?*" — and she repeated the swift and broken passage.

"He says he played in the Glasgow orchestra under Manns," I ventured.

"That would be Augustus Manns; he was a good musician; my own father played for him at the Crystal Palace."

"Donald *beag* seems to have had experience before he came to Orwell," I said to complete the incident.

"I would not put it past him," the Master's wife concluded. "They say he has had seven wives, and some of them yet living." But she always affected to believe it was Pat Bolger who had been making the music.

XX

THE TWO PRINCES

THIS same singer sang three songs as part of an elaborate entertainment that was given to the Prince of Wales in that far place. With exquisite depreciation of his own knowledge, the Prince expressed surprise at such excellence in a place whose musical achievements had hitherto escaped his attention. In the spirit of the opera, she knelt before him, and as he took her by the hand, she protested that she "had never been off the Island." This was a traditional jest in which she had been duly instructed.

American visitors come to this place with a preconceived notion that all the natives are simple. They cannot distinguish between peoples who do not speak their own language. They classify them all as foreigners. They are not concerned with the distinctions these natives may have set up between themselves. One of these tourists on the road accosted a handsome well-bred boy, newly graduated from an important university.

"What is your trade ? " he asked.

"I am a saddler, sir," the boy replied.

In the Island there is a long tradition of high birth, and when the Prince appeared, his appearance was as natural as the appearance of the sun above the horizon. This Island was the last refuge of the feudal system. It was originally divided into sixty-seven lots of 20,000 acres each; and these estates were assigned to a corresponding number of important and high-born personages in England, with the obligation to place emigrants upon them. Some of these landlords visited their estates, and to this day one will be shown in an old house the very spot where one of those mighty persons sat. They brought with them their relatives. The Governors brought aides, justices, and secretaries. Some of these remained, to live in reflected or intrinsic glory, and gave to the place a sense of dignity and style. In addition, the Highland immigrants brought with them their own sense of particularity based upon the practice of the clan. Not Debrett nor Burke could excel the Master's wife in appraising the present value of these old distinctions.

In a community, therefore, in which all lived in daily intercourse with the descendants of those important persons, although now sadly fallen from their high estate, there was little alarm over the arrival of the Prince. There is yet a sense of style an ease. When the Lieutenant-Governor honours one with a visit, he comes with his chauffeur and footman in livery, with the arms of the province emblazoned on the doors of his car. Professor Whitnall informs me that a like spirit prevails in Oxford. A Mahatma applied for admission to Christ's. When the Dean was informed that a Mahatma was a reincarnation of the Son, he declined to receive him, on the ground that "the undergraduates would never stand it." He was recommended to apply to Magdalen. The President of that particular College made no difficulty; he would accept him even if he were a reincarnation of the Father; he had had the Prince of Wales the year before. Likewise, King Edward, when he was Prince, had been on the Island.

When the Prince of Wales visited Canada in the summer of 1920, he landed first in the Maritime provinces. The *Renown* lay in the splendid harbour of Charlottetown. The dock was thronged with people. Awnings had been erected and red carpets laid. When the Prince came up the gangway in his fair beauty, he appeared to come as a glorious creature fresh risen from the morning sea.

To the Highlanders of Catholic memory he was the Bonnie Prince from over the Water; to many a woman he was her own soldier son who never came home again. One old man with tears streaming down his weathered face — early as it was, he had been drinking for the occasion — was quietly going through the litany of his oaths: "I fought for his father, I fought for his grandfather, I fought for his great-grandmother; and, by God, I would like to strike a blow for that little fellow too." A judicious woman observed, "That young man must have been well brought up."

Chief-Justice Mathieson, who at the moment was also acting Lieutenant-Governor, had issued invitations to a reception, and the Master's wife was included in the number, himself being dead. She announced firmly that she would attend. This

resolution, we all believed, merely arose out of a further resolution to have a new dress made — for the
last time. For many years she had in the house a
length of heavy black poplin, ribbed and lustrous with
silk and flax, which she received from a son who had
passion for rich fabrics.

The presence of the Prince was held to be
sufficient warrant for converting the fabric into a
garment; but the task was not easy. Local skill was
inadequate. If the material were entrusted to an
establishment in the town, there was no surety that
it would not be wasted, or all the remnants returned.
In the end she decided to go to the town for a week,
and engage an artist who would work in her own
room under her very eye. She was determined also
that the dress "should be high in the neck and with
long sleeves." This was to be her final protest against
the prevalent fashion.

We had at the time — and still have — at Orwell
a carriage, known as a victoria or more correctly
and in derision as a barouche, that is, a four-wheeled
low vehicle with folding top, two inside seats facing
each other, and a high front seat for the driver. This
carriage came to the place some twenty years before
when motor cars in other places made horses obsolete;
but with its rubber tires, morocco leather, and blue
cloth was yet a sumptuous affair. It could be drawn
by two horses, but the nature of the roads prescribed
a single draught.

There was a horse corresponding with the weight
and beauty of the carriage. Her name was Gipsy II.

How she came to Orwell, and how it came about that she was driven by Barrett, all those years of war her friend and mine, in the barouche that carried guests to the reception of the Prince of Wales — all this is contained in the army records.

The Master's wife by reason of her age and tall strength — she was then nearly eighty-five — excited some interest. The new dress in itself would have made her remarkable. The black poplin was adorned with embroidered silk, another household treasure, and she herself described the whole effect as "a regal robe." As the Prince was about to leave he turned and spoke with her again, and came away laughing. I asked what the Prince had said to her, and warned her of the traditional lightness of speech between princes and women.

"I am not going to tell," was her only answer.

"Then what did you say to him, as he came away laughing ? " I asked again.

"I just said to him, as I would say to one of yourselves, 'Good-bye, Dear.' "

On the way home she remarked with a touch of old acerbity, "The last time the Prince of Wales was here, it was your aunt Janet who went with your father." That was sixty years ago. Now it was clear why she herself persisted in going this time. She died the following year.

At a very early age I had formed the design of marrying a well-grown young woman upon her invitation. In preparation for the new way of life I built a house of snow, and gathered birch bark for

THE MASTER'S WIFE

a fire; but I lacked a costume suitable for the ceremonial. I asked the Master for his "military cap and sword." This cap was a splendid affair with a plume of black feathers. His military career, I learned much later, was confined to a militia company in which he was lieutenant; but the plumed cap suggests that he must have been transferred to the staff, possibly as paymaster, for his accounts are yet in existence. There is also extant his "manual of musketry drill," written in his own hand, and probably copied from an official source. I never saw him in uniform, but often heard him repeat old commands in a loud musical tone, as part of a narrative. The command that astonished most was, "Prepare to meet the cavalry."

In the year 1860, he formed part of the guard of honour that received the Prince of Wales in Charlottetown. New uniforms were required for the event, but the tailors were overwhelmed with work. The War Office merely issued the blue cloth, and left the forces free to make their own garments. His wife undertook the work for him. A tailor, Sandy Stewart, by name, who lived some miles away, agreed to cut the long tunic and supervise the sewing. She went to his shop every morning and sewed all day. She often pointed out the shop and the Enman house where she had her dinner. The blue coat with red piping was duly finished in time for the parade, but for some domestic reason it was her sister-in-law, not herself, who witnessed the spectacle. Now, at last, the old grievance was allayed.

XXI

THE SPIRIT OF WAR

ONE afternoon early in August, 1914, I was sitting with the Master's wife on a long wooden bench that stands in shelter of a green wall dividing the farm-yard from the house, lawn, and garden. This wall was a grievance to her. It obscured her view of the conduct of the persons within. The bench was from the old church. Its place was below the pulpit, and it had always been occupied by the most important section of the elders, each in his appointed seat, the Master amongst them. Dorothy of the dedication was sitting between us. She was reading *The Oxford Book of English Verse.*

The book had been given to me by Henry Frowde of the Oxford University Press. This collection of verse, the best chosen and in itself the noblest in any language, was made by Sir A. T. Quiller-Couch. I was so interested in the book when it first appeared that I made a textual study of it as a scholar would, and sent in writing to Mr. Frowde, at his request, the result of my observations. He thought well to send the letter to the author, who was pleased to write that he would make certain emendations in future editions. His letter began with old Daniel's lines :

And for my part, if only one allow
The pain my lab'ring spirit takes in this,
He is to me a theatre large enow
And his applause only sufficient is ...

This letter, with its generous sentiments and
delicate characters, in a brown envelope has always
lain in the book as the most convenient place to
preserve it. In some obscure way this book with the
associated letter is bound up in my remembrance of
the War. It was with me at the beginning; it remained
with me until the end. The child laid down the open
book upon the bench. I picked it up and read where
she had been reading :

It is not to be thought of that the flood
    Of British freedom, which, to the open sea
Of the world's praise, from dark antiquity
Hath flow'd 'with pomp of waters, unwithstood' ...
    That this most famous stream in bogs and sands
        Should perish; and to evil and to good
        Be lost for ever ...

A carriage drawn by two horses drove in with
some visitors. I asked the young man to put away
the horses. He was sorry. He could not wait.
England had declared war upon Germany. They
went on their way to the town. The next place I met
the young man was at Neuville St. Vaast, and the
other occupant of the carriage at Bailleul. The news
spread through the house and garden. Jeffrey, also
of the dedication, picked up the book, and read for a
moment in it.

"I am going to the War," he said.

"Are you going to-night or in the morning?" I asked him.

"It will be a long war," he answered, "and I don't think they will miss me much if I wait until morning." He went away in the morning. I saw him for a moment at Valcartier, next at Ploegstreet for a whole winter.

A brother, who also spends his summers at Orwell, went to the telegraph office. In the morning he was gone too. He was, I understood, in the militia. Papers franked through the post would be coming. There was in his room a jacket with a crown upon the sleeve. I met him also at Valcartier, next at le Romarin, and at many other strange places during the succeeding years. In time the official papers were addressed Colonel ——, C.M.G., D.S.O.

Amidst the sudden movement the Master's wife only said, "Dear, dear," and spent her time reading the Hebrew prophecies and the Apocalypse. Any passage suitable to the occasion she would read aloud. By these she governed her moods, and foretold the incidents, course, and duration of the War. Sihon was Belgium: And I sent messengers unto Sihon with words of peace, saying, Let me pass through thy land. I will go along by the highway, I will neither turn unto the right hand nor to the left. Thou shalt sell me meat for money, that I may eat, and give me water for money, that I may drink; only I will pass through on my feet.

Moab was Germany: We have heard of the

pride of Moab, his loftiness, and his arrogance, and his pride and the haughtiness of his heart. I know his wrath; but it shall not be so; his lies shall not so effect it. A sword is upon the liars; a sword is upon her mighty men, and they shall be dismayed. For the Lord God of recompense shall surely requite.

The German Kaiser and the Austrian emperor were clearly "the Eagle." Was not that very bird emblazoned on their escutcheons? Thou hast afflicted the meek, thou hast hurt the peaceable, thou hast loved liars, thou hast destroyed the dwellings of such as did thee no harm. Therefore is thy wrongful dealing come up unto the Highest, and thy pride unto the Mighty. And I saw, and behold, the whole body of the Eagle was burned.

Although she did not read German, she knew that *Der Tag* meant The Day, and she read in her book : Alas for the Day; for the Day of the Lord is at hand. Woe unto you that desire the Day; the Day is darkness and not light; As if a man did flee from a lion, and a bear met him. In this she found guidance to the fate of Germany between England and Russia.

Her most subtle exegesis was directed towards an understanding of the relation between the various parts of the British Empire, but, as I afterwards learned, it was not until the Canadians were engaged at Ypres and the Australians had destroyed the *Emden* that the whole matter was revealed to her, and then only by collating various passages : The lion has roared, who will not fear? What is thy mother? A lioness : she lay down among lions.

And she brought up one of her whelps; it became a young lion, and it learned to catch the prey in the islands of the sea. And every ship-master, and all the company in ships, and sailors, and as many as trade with the enemy by sea stood afar off. Thy mother is like a vine in thy blood, planted by the waters; she was fruitful and full of branches by reason of many waters. She calculated the length of the War would be "forty and two months," and she was not far astray.

Shortly after the outbreak of war, news came that a young man had died in his bed. She had just seen her own sons and grandsons off to the War. She opened her book, and quietly gave it to her informant to read : Weep not for the dead, neither bemoan him; but weep more for him that goeth away; for he shall return no more, nor see his native country. In this her prophecy was wrong. All did return, but not until nearly five years had passed. And they brought back certain distinctions; but the old habit of reticence and dislike of emotion was so strong upon her that she never could bring herself to make a word of mention — certainly not in our hearing.

War was not for women, and she disapproved, openly at least, of her granddaughter's conduct, when she crossed the ocean to join the Red Cross in England. She was "lonesome for her men." The peril of the sea was at the worst. Two of her young friends had perished on the *Lusitania*. To appease her grandmother she put forward as a defence that she "was a good swimmer." She was a good swimmer.

She once swam across the harbour of Hamilton in Bermuda, a distance of three quarters of a mile — and back again.

Even in that remote place the idea of war was long familiar. The Master's wife as a child, had seen two opposing forces of Highlanders and Irish marching with flags to an election and the consequent riot. Her uncle's house was used as a dressing-station; and in the morning she saw "the dead lying with their hair matted to the floor in their frozen blood." Our immediate neighbour, a very old man, had served in the Peninsular War. He was known as "the pensioner." He had been shot through the body and "crawled behind a fence to die." As he was disappointed in his immediate purpose he took means to ascertain the nature and extent of his wound. For purpose of prognosis he decided to drink some water, and if the water ran out at the wound he would then decide that any further efforts were useless. He drank, and the water did not issue from his body.

The grandmother was a girl of fifteen when Waterloo was fought. Her two uncles, Andrew and John, were "surgeons" in the army. When night fell they had "legs and arms piled up like cordwood," the result of their amputations. The elder of the two, whose name was conferred upon me, had a bullet through his ankle; and ever afterwards when he rode his horse he carried a bottle of water which he would pour down his boot to ease the pain of the old wound. On the night of the battle she herself in Scotland saw "the scarlet troops marching and counter-marching on the sky."

The Crimean War and the Indian Mutiny were familiar to us by reason of two pensioners who justified their meagre allowance, and also supplemented it, by narratives of the events in which they had a share. The Crimean War was considered to have been a dull affair, because the local historian was a dull fellow; for it is quite true that, whils it is soldiers who make wars, it is historians who make the history of them.

But the Indian veteran made the Mutiny shine with all the splendour of the Indian sun. The Master would believe anything he was told, provided he had read something on the subject; and he had a book on the Mutiny with coloured plates. One of the pictures of which he highly approved bore the legend, *Mutineers blown from the Cannon's Mouth.* This old soldier was free of the house for a week at a time, and his artistry was inexhaustible.

"Did you ever kill a man ? " I whispered to him, astonished at my own boldness. The veteran turned a grateful eye upon me.

"With my own hand ? " he reflected with judicial impartiality. One would think it was the first time the question had ever presented itself to him. As if he were meditating upon a deep problem, he set forth the premisses :

He was riding beside his General, "bridle to bridle." They were "under fire" from a fort upon a hill; horses and men were falling.

"Munro," the General asked, "How far away is that fort ? "

"Fourteen hundred and forty-two yards, sir." The General claimed it was fifteen hundred.

"Let me put it to the test, sir." The General agreed.

"I laid a gun at 1442 yards. I gave the order, 'Fire.' The fort was silenced." They rode forward to inspect the result of that single shot, and found seventy-five dead men.

"Of course," he added judiciously, "I did not pull the lanyard with my own hand." Like all artists, he stopped short of the categorical answer.

The Fenian Raid was made vivid by an old woman who confided to the public that she always slept with a pitchfork in her bed. I was six years old at the time of the Franco-Prussian War. A certain neighbour would come every week on the arrival of the newspapers to hear the news; and I was careful to listen unseen to the reading and the comments that were made. I could read quite well for myself, but children were denied access to the newspapers. The neighbour called the invaders "Prooshians," and I thought the Master went too far in complaisance by adopting that form of speech. I was aware that he knew better. The most deadly critic is the conscience of a child.

When the war of 1914 broke out, local opinion was calm. One neighbour was unmoved by the invasion of Belgium. He thought it "a bad thing interfering in another man's business." This was an affair between two neighbours. Another man was sure that "war would make good prices," and he recited his remembrance of the American Civil War. John Macqueen depended upon the Navy. He was certain the German ships would "hide in the creeks."

Upon matters of the sea this man spoke with authority, for he spent his summers fishing as far away as St. Peter's Island. "The sea is an element in itself," he said. Upon one trip he had as crew a man from Green-Marsh, which is six miles inland, and he could teach him nothing; whereas "a boy from Point Prim would know it was high tide even if he was sleeping in his bed." He had little respect for German seamanship, and the utmost he feared was that "they might do some mischief out of mere stupidity." Upon the whole he was convinced that "those foreigners should not be allowed to have ships at all." When the War was over he admitted that there was one subject on which he desired information. The problem that troubled him was, how they manoeuvered an army; and I took upon myself the function of Munro.

Probably no person in the world was more fully informed upon the events of the War than the Master's wife. From one informant she had a continuous account in sonnet form. To those who did not choose to go overseas she applied his bitter line : Enslave ourselves to keep our masters free. From another she had specific observation of the domestic economy and agricultural practice of the various European countries traversed by the army, illustrated by a blade or ear of wheat, a lock of wool, a shoot, a flower, or seed according to the season, and a comparison with her own of their methods in tilling the ground, planting the seed, reaping the harvest, baking bread, fashioning garments, or preparing a pig for food. Two things she would not believe, that a dog could be trained to operate a churn, that a horse might be used for meat.

In her garden she had a "rose of Valois." A grandson discerning that he was actually in the district of Valois found some authentic roses in a tangled thicket. With his bayonet he dug out a root and sent it to her in a cigarette box. She planted the root, nurtured the reviving plant; but she never lived to see it bloom. Another grandson was very dear to her. From childhood he would run upon her secret errands, drive a horse, or weed a garden. A shell came into his company, "like a shot into a flock of plover in little Angus' field." He was wounded in the foot, and a minute fragment of metal pierced his side over the heart. He refused to have the missile removed. He had now a valid excuse against his grandmother's exactions; he could walk lame, and allow her to feel the piece of shell under the skin of his breast.

But most of all, she liked to hear of military operations in language she could understand : "The enemy were entrenched on the ridge behind Dundee, their right resting on the Vernon at Glencoe, their left at the head of the Montague. Our lines ran from the church to the half-way house." Then would

follow mention of the relative places where each one
she knew was engaged. When Sir Archibald
Macdonell, who had commanded the 1st Division,
came to Orwell, looked upon the scene, and read the
details, he recognized at once the dispositions for
Vimy Ridge.

XXII

FALSE PRIDE

How real and firmly founded was the family tradition we did not suspect. The Master knew, but he concealed the knowledge, lest it might minister to the spirit of pride in his own heart, and, worse still, engender a false pride in the minds of his children. Against that sin he was ever alert, and he missed no means of abasing the spirit of pride. He had no collateral relations of his own, who might serve his purpose; but he found enough in his wife's long descent; and these he was careful to present as "cousins of your own," even if it were of the third or fourth degree. This particularity was a cause of extreme irritation to his wife.

To one who came upon the matter in the books, it was something of a discovery. In a work of erudition, common in any library, the history of the Clan Chattan is recorded from documents as authentic as historical documents ever are. This Clan included eighteen septs, of which the Macphails were the 14th, and they took protection of the Mackintosh in the year 1500. In the Kinrara *History of the Mackintoshes* one reads that in the time of Duncan the 8th, 1456-1496, lived "Paul Gow, good sir (grand sire) of Sir Andrew Macphail, the priest, of whom the Clan had their beginning."

This Sir Andrew wrote the third of the three histories of Clan Chattan, upon which Kinrara in part founded his work. It began with the 1st Mackintosh, and ended with William 15th murdered at Strathbogie in 1550. According to the records, "Macphail of Inverairnie, the chief of that ancient tribe of Clan Chattan," finally acquired Inverairnie in 1631, but not without strife. As early as 1496, more than a century before, "the tribe was pursued by Dunbar for the space of one year last bye past, for the wrongous occupation and labouring of the lands." The original grant by which they acquired a heritable right is dated May 19, 1631, whereby the reputed owner "in respect of a thousand pounds scots granted a wadset right and long tack of Inverairnie."

The subsequent history of the estate is recorded in the deeds. On March 13th, 1689, the reversionary rights were secured by a grandson "in respect of a feu duty of 209 marks and other presentations." They passed through a series — Paul, John, William, Robert, Alexander. This last, overburdened by payments to relatives, was in 1743 compelled to mortgage the estate, but he redeemed it in 1756. Out of this transaction he never emerged. In his struggle to maintain his position, he executed a transfer to a relative. The deed is drawn in his own hand, dated April 14th, 1763, and is witnessed by three cousins, John, Robert and Donald. Litigation followed and lasted for ten years. In the end Alexander not only lost his estate but found himself in prison. His pursuers were John Macpherson of Ballackroan, and Farquhar MacGillivray. According to the historians of the Clan Chattan, "There were no two more determined and unscrupulous men in the County of Inverness," which is saying a good deal.

From his prison Alexander Macphail immediately sent a petition to Sheriff Macqueen demanding release. In this petition he recites, "that notwithstanding his having settled with Dunmaglass, Farquhar MacGillivray of Dalcrombie, without having any special mandate from the said Captain William MacGillivray, who is out of the kingdom in Georgia, upon Monday 1st, the 6th current (Dec. 1773) came with a party of 12 men armed with guns and staves, and upon the high road attacked the petitioner, and by the strong hand held him about two hours in the snow, by force and violence, without having a caption or any warrant, or messenger or officer of the law with him, and had him conveyed to prison." The sheriff on the 9th, ordered answer within forty-eight hours. By a notation — dated the 13th, and still on the paper, no answer was received, and Alexander was released. But the estate was lost to the family forever.

From the beginning, the Macphails appear on the records as ecclesiastics. In 1574 Andrew was reader at Petty and Bracklie, at Kirkhill in 1575, at Kingussie in 1581, at ᴦores in 1590. In a deed drawn at Inverness 26th April, 1595, two of the witnesses are

Andrew Macphail, Minister of the Word of God at Croy, and Severinus Macphail, Minister of the Church at Petty. This last under the name of Souverane had been presented by James VI to Alvie in 1585, where he continued for nine years.

In the kirkyard of Daviot, seven miles from Inverness, is a flat stone to the memory of Rev. James Macphail, for 37 years Minister, who died in 1839 in the 73rd year of his age. This one and his brother William, who was Minister of the Scottish Church in Rotterdam, were sons of Rev. Hector Macphail, a native of Inverness, M.A., King's College, Aberdeen 1737, and Minister of Resolis, 1748-74. His grandson, Rev. Hector William, gained the gold medal for classics at the Royal Academy, Inverness in 1835, and died only in 1897. He also is buried in Daviot.

I first saw Inverairnie in the spring of 1917. I had been recalled to London to give the Cavendish lecture. The theme was "A Day's Work" — at Vimy Ridge, and I was presumed to be so exhausted by the effort that I was given two weeks leave. With "Dorothy" I went to Inverness, and on to Nairn where we lived in the house of a good woman, Mrs. Simpson. I was very tired, and for much of the time lay in bed. In the room was a set of the *Edinburgh Review* from the year 1802, and of the *Quarterly* from a few years later. I began with the numbers of exactly one hundred years previous, and continued reading until I was rested. They were even more interesting than the current numbers. Early in the morning when my leave was up, the child was saying good-bye to me on the stairs. She missed a step, fell, and broke her ankle. I heard the bone snap, but the train was due, and I was compelled to leave her lying where she fell. But she was amply cared for by those good Highland people.

One day we walked in Nairn, and on our return, Mrs. Simpson asked if by chance we had found any of my own people. I said we had not looked for them. "Perhaps it might be as well not," was her shrewd comment. But we did call upon Mr. George Bain, editor of *The Telegraph*, who had high repute for his local knowledge. He knew of none bearing the name. Suddenly he became vague and mysterious. The child, suspecting there was something to be said improper for her hearing, allowed she had some shopping to do, and would return. Mr. Bain, being assured I was prepared for the worst, made this disclosure : "You may not be aware that your people were Episcopalians."

He knew his neighbour, The Macintosh, very well; his son Captain Angus Macintosh who had just married Lady Maud, daughter of the Duke of Devonshire, he knew slightly; but he had "heard that he had married into rather a goodish English family." Lady Maud, to whom I afterwards mentioned this too moderate appraisement of her family expressed no surprise. She had been well schooled in the Highland doctrine of family preeminence.

We made an excursion to Inverairnie, some ten miles up the river from Nairn. We were received most cordially by the *de facto* owner. When I told him my name, he knew me at once; he had read his title-deeds. I had already been informed that his name was Smithson, an Englishman, a cousin two or three times removed from the Duke of Northumberland. His delicacy was too subtle for words. He might have been born and bred Highland. He brought liquor as fine and as quick as any Highlander could. He treated me as if I were the *de jure* owner, although he did admit in answer to a question that his father had bought the place from the MacGillivrays in 1867 for the sum of sixty thousand pounds sterling. He would not drink until I had poured for him. He came to see me in Montreal.

On the return from Inverairnie Dorothy betrayed her suspicion that there may have been some secret dealings over the liquor. She took the offensive from afar off. She said she had climbed a hill, and as far as the eye could reach there was nothing but moor, and crag, and fen; that there was not more than four hundred acres of good land on the whole place; that Mrs. Smithson had told her she could not make a vegetable garden, as the deer came down from the hills in the springtime and ate every green plant. In the end I asked boldly how she would like to live there. She merely surmised "It might be a little quiet in winter."

With the loss of the lands the coherence of the family was destroyed. The larger part drifted southward, and took root in Argyllshire, where they became absorbed into the general life of the Lowlands, and lost the sense of relationship. Nearly all of those who now bear the name look no further back than this new home. The remnant that remained in the Highlands carried on the tradition of scholarship and particularity, and then died out, so that not one of the name now remains. Two emigrants went to Australia in 1852; at times a letter would arrive from that far place. One descendant was known to be alive in Australia in the year 1897.

The great-grandfather's only brother, Hugh, it was known, went to "the States," and was lost to sight for sixty years. In 1907 I was upon a journey to California by the route that passes through the Arizona desert. There was a train-wreck, and when the journey was resumed, a sense of intimacy had developed among the passengers. In those days liquor was sold on the trains like any other commodity. I observed in the smoking car a man with whom I discerned an instant affinity. He was a solid man, rather formally dressed, with a grave massive face. I asked him to share a drink with me. He agreed; and presently, according to the American custom, he produced a card on which his name was engraved, Alexander Macphail. He was first cousin to the Master, his only relative in America.

This tradition of scholarship, after a long resting stage, was revived in the Master's family. Of his ten children, seven attained University degrees of various kinds, arts, medicine, science; and two others a collegiate rank that entitled them to engage in the immemorial practice of teaching school. But to his mild regret, none qualified, formally at least, for the ministry. This delinquency was to him a reproach, as if in some way he had failed in his duty.

At this point, so near the end, it is right to meet the just reproach of any reader who by chance may read these pages, that the creature is magnified at the expense of the creator, the writer at the expense of the subject with a shamelessness, it may be alleged, proper only to those who are already famous or already dead. Such reader is reminded of the vastly more that might be said, and with hard reticence is not. And if I have merely created an image, the ancient defence remains : An image makes us know, love, remember. But the final defence is the defence of Hroswitha of Gandersheim, now in her Benedictine grave these nine hundred years : *Si enim alicui placet mea devotio, gaudebo : si autem nulli placet : memet ipsam tamen iuvat quod feci.* If this devotion gives pleasure to others, I shall be glad; but even if no one is pleased, I myself had pleasure in the doing of it.

THE END.

EXPLANATORY NOTES
for *The Master's Wife*, Third Edition

page

1 l. 1

"He" - William McPhail (1830-1905); see Ian Ross Robertson, "William McPhail," *Dictionary of Canadian Biography*, Vol. XIII (Toronto, 1994), pp. 671-2

"she" - Mrs. William McPhail (1834-1920), *née* Catherine Elizabeth Smith

16 l. 10

"John McCrae" - John McCrae (1872-1918), physician and poet, author of *In Flanders Fields*, colleague in medicine of Andrew Macphail at McGill University, and a member of the first editorial committee of *The University Magazine*, edited by Macphail. After his death, Macphail published a 95-page tribute as an accompaniment to a collection of McCrae's verse. See "John McCrae: An Essay in Character," in McCrae, *In Flanders Fields and other Poems* (Toronto, 1919). Many of the 29 poems in the book had appeared first in *The University Magazine*.

24 para. 3, l. 6

"Williams" - Sir Dawson Williams (1854-1928), editor of the *British Medical Journal* from 1898 to 1928

26 l. 11

"William" - William McPhail (1802-52)

26 para. 2, l. 3

"ago" - By 1927 Macphail was writing this book.

28 para. 2, l. 7

"Macpherson" - Mrs. William McPhail (1804-88), *née* Mary Macpherson

32 para. 2, l. 7

"University" - Rev John Hugh McKerras (1832-80), born at Nairn, Scotland, educated at Queen's (BA 1850, MA 1852), professor of classical literature at Queen's, 1864-80

33 para. 3, l. 4

"descendant" - Jeffrey Macphail (1894-1947), only son of Andrew Macphail

37 para. 2, l. 1

"Mavor" - James Mavor (1854-1925), Scottish political economist who taught at the University of Toronto, 1892-1923; member of the editorial committee of *The University Magazine*, 1907-16

51 para. 2, l. 8

"Peters" - James Horsfield Peters (*ca.* 1811- 91), Judge of the Supreme Court of Prince Edward Island, 1848-91; although respected as a highly competent jurist, he also had a reputation for severity in sentencing; see Ian Ross Robertson, "James Horsfield Peters," *Dictionary of Canadian Biography*, Vol. XII (Toronto, 1990), pp. 838-42, and p. 72 in the present text.

53 l. 1

"Jongers" - Alphonse Jongers, French-born portrait artist, whose portrait of Andrew Macphail in 1924 is the frontispiece to this book, and whose portrait of William McPhail, the Master, in 1899, faces page 52.

53 para. 3, l. 2

"Leacock" - Stephen Leacock (1869-1944), English-born political economist and humourist who taught at McGill University, 1903-36. Probably Macphail's closest friend among his academic colleagues, Leacock was on the first editorial committee of *The University Magazine*. Leacock's obituary article in tribute to Macphail is a splendid evocation of his personality; see "Andrew Macphail," *Queen's Quarterly*, XLV (Winter 1938), 445-52.

54 para. 2, 1. 1

"McKenzie" - Robert Tait McKenzie (1867- 1938), physician and sculptor, Macphail's roommate in his student days at McGill in the 1880s

58 para. 2, 1. 1

"Premier" - William Wilfred Sullivan (1843-1920), premier of Prince Edward Island, 1879-89, provincial chief justice, 1889-1917

77 1. 4

"Dyonnet" - Edmond Dyonnet (1859-1954), French-born painter, resident in Montreal, and a member of the Pen and Pencil Club, to which Macphail, McCrae, Leacock, and Jongers also belonged

88 para. 3, 1. 5

"Grey" - Albert Henry George Grey, fourth Earl (1851-1917), governor-general of Canada, 1904-11. Lucy Maud Montgomery was invited to Orwell to meet Grey in 1910, and for her comments, see Mary Rubio and Elizabeth Waterston, eds., *The Selected Journals of L.M. Montgomery, Volume II: 1910-1921* (Toronto, 1987), pp. 10-17.

118 para. 3, 1. 5

"Old Gentleman" - Edward William Thomson (1849-1924), author and journalist, one of Macphail's most intimate friends

122 1. 11

"English" - Alexander Anderson; see pp. 177 *et seq.*

126 1. 9

"Donald MacDonald" - Rev Donald McDonald (1783-1867), native of Scotland who moved to Prince Edward

Island in the late 1820s and founded a group of Calvinists unique to the colony, known as the McDonaldites. In McDonald's own time they identified themselves as Kirkmen, and they presently call themselves members of the Free Church of Scotland. See David Weale, "Donald McDonald," *Dictionary of Canadian Biography,* Vol. IX (Toronto, 1976), pp. 480-1.

129 para. 4, 1. 3

"Colonel" - James Alexander Macphail (1870-1949), younger brother of Macphail, usually known as "Alexander"; a poet and professor of engineering at Queen's University, 1904-39

162 para. 3, 1. 1

"Macdonell" - Sir Archibald Macdonell (1864-1941)

177 para. 2, 1. 4

"Anderson" - Alexander Anderson, born and educated in Scotland, professor at Prince of Wales College, 1862-1901, and principal, 1868-1901. In 1888 McGill University gave him the recognition of an honorary degree.

180 para. 2, 1. 4

"Caven" - John Caven, professor at Prince of Wales College, 1879-1901

180 para. 3, 1. 7

Lepage - Thomas Lepage, professor at Prince of Wales College, intermittently between 1876 and his death in 1889

188 para. 2, 1. 22

he - R. Tait McKenzie

198 para. 2, 1. 3

"Chief-Justice" - John Alexander Mathieson (1863-1947), a classmate of Macphail at Prince of Wales College, a teacher in the neighbouring village of

Kensington when Macphail taught in Malpeque, premier of Prince Edward Island, 1911-17, and provincial chief justice, 1917-43

199 l. 1

"Adami" - J.G. Adami (1862-1926), English-born professor of pathology at McGill, 1892-1919

206 l. 1

"brother" - James Alexander Macphail

206 para. 2, l. 1

"Byng" - Viscount Julian Byng (1862-1935), commander of the Canadian Corps in the First World War, 1916-17, and governor-general of Canada, 1921-26

226 l. 2

"Barrett" - Macphail's batman when overseas in the First World War

230 para. 4, l. 1

"brother" - James Alexander Macphail

232 para. 3, l. 2

"granddaughter" - Mrs. Dorothy Lindsay (1897-1988), *née* Dorothy Macphail, only daughter of Andrew Macphail

233 para. 2, l. 4

"riot" - the Belfast riot of 1 March 1847, which resulted in at least three deaths; see H.T. Holman, "The Belfast, Riot," *The Island Magazine*, No. 14 (Fall-Winter 1983), pp. 3-7

236 para. 3, l. 3

"informant" - James Alexander Macphail

236 para. 3, l. 7

"another" - Andrew Macphail

CORRIGENDA

page

53   fourth line from the bottom of the page: "stalemate" is all one word

70   para. 2, line 4: "dammed" rather than "damned"

71   para. 2, line 6: there should be commas after "thought" and after "word"

95   para. 2, line 8: "apotheosis" - the second "o" has been left out

96   line 3: "femininity" rather than "feminity"

128   para. 3, line 8: "*agu's cuir a mach an cu*"

134   para. 3, line 7: "strippings" rather than "striplings"

140   para. 2, line 9: "contrition" rather than "contribution"

156   line 6: "his" rather than "this" convenience

174   line 1: "to" rather than "in"

180   para. 2, line 4: "Caven" rather than "Gaven"

181   fourth last line of the poem: "light" should have a capital "L"

184   third last line: "Keir" rather than "Kier"

203   para. 2, line 2: "on" rather than "an"

203   last line of the page: either "was" should have been made "were" or "reasons" made singular

223   para. 2, line 6: should begin with "and" rather than "an"

Incorrect Dates And Ages

page

26   last line of para. 1: "1833" rather than "1832"
27   para. 2, line 1: the age was "fifty" rather than "fifty-two
31   para. 2, line 11: "1833" rather than "1832"
33   para. 2, line 1: "1844" rather than "1838"
224 para. 2, line 2: "1919" rather than "1920"